The Sigil Self

A Journey of Self Discovery to Reveal Your Cosmic Signature

by David Burman

Curio Hut Press

Published by Curio Hut Press

www.curiohut.com

Printed in the United States of America

Print Edition

First Edition - 2025

ISBN: 979-8-9995303-2-5

Cover, Text and Design by David Burman

This book is intended for informational and spiritual purposes only.
It is not a substitute for professional advice or treatment.

Table of Contents

Sevenfold Invocation

A book of revelation

But never condemnation

Discover not a verdict

The Sigil's a reflection

It belongs to only you

Unique and your own design

That speaks through symbol and sign

Now let's recognize your strengths

Face your shadows without fear

Finish this with head held high

Full of confidence and pride

You are designed not random

A child of the Cosmos

Claim your place among the stars

-David Burman
Creator of The Sigil Self

A note from the Author

Introduction

It's recommended that you finish the introduction to get familiar with the system before starting your calculations and Sigil creation. A guided Walkthrough begins after the Introduction. When you're ready, the Cosmic Signature and Numerology Worksheets are on page 114-115 or download them at curiohut.com

What Is the Sigil Self?

Through guided exploration, you will uncover your Cosmic Signature. A unique Sigil created from your own identity. The Cosmic Signature is not something you choose, it's a Sigil you reveal.

Your Cosmic Signature is both a visual and energetic reflection of you, a sacred mark drawn from your individuality. This is not an abstract concept, it's a personal map formed from the numerology of your name and birth date.

As you pass through the eight revelations called Stations, each one decodes a truth and unlocks a coordinate on a 9x9 sacred square. Line by line, your Cosmic Signature takes form. It will ultimately reveal The Sigil Self.

The Sigil Self: Fusion of Esoteric Systems

The Sigil Self draws upon several different esoteric disciplines, each contributing a deep layer of insight. When woven together, they reveal a multi-dimensional portrait of the self.

Pythagorean Numerology - Every Station in the Sigil Self begins with the numbers encoded in your name and birth date. Based on the Pythagorean System, each letter is assigned a number from 1 to 9. These numbers carry vibration, meaning and pattern. They transform mundane data into meaningful spiritual codes. The logic of numerology anchors the system with precision and repeatability, allowing anyone to follow the path and uncover their hidden structure.

Sigil Magic - At the core of the Sigil Self is the craft of Sigil Making, transforming intention into symbol. Unlike traditional Sigils, these are created as magical representations of your personal and spiritual blueprint. As you move through the stations, your Sigil takes shape, guided by number and meaning. The final result is a unique Sigil that holds the energy of your self discovery, your Cosmic Signature.

Sacred Geometry and Grid Magic - As the fragments of your sigil are revealed they are plotted on a 9x9 grid, echoing the magic square, the numerological matrix, and the mystical nature of number-based design. Sacred Geometry gives form to the intangible, grounding your insights within a structure. The grid is both a map and a mirror - it reflects your path while also adding a shape to The Cosmic Signature.

Archetypal Wisdom - This system includes a full pantheon of 9 Archetypes, each representing a core path of identity. As you progress you will encounter subtypes that build a rich archetypal ecosystem paralleling myth and story.

Astrological Influence - The Sigil Self uses your birth timing - month, day and year and integrates it into the numerological process. In this system, astrology isn't used as signs and houses, but as vibrations translated through number.

Name Magic - Names hold power. In this system, your first, middle and last names are each examined through numerology to uncover the gifts and traits woven into your identity. Whether it's your chosen name or the name given to you at birth, each one carries a thread in the web of your soul's design.

Initiatory Pathworking - The structure of the eight Stations is a journey through the layers of the self. The Sigil Self unfolds in a cycle of roots, trials, virtues and transcendence. You're not just learning about yourself, you are becoming yourself.

How to Use this Book

As you move through each station you will:

- Use the Cosmic Signature and Numerology Worksheets to find your X and Y answers
- Learn what each station reveals and consult to the Reference Section to explore further
- Plot a coordinate on your grid and draw Sigil lines using the Cosmic Signature Worksheet

Each discovery is mapped on the 9x9 grid - a sacred square that's the key to uncovering your Sigil. This Sigil is built step by step, a visual reflection of your Cosmic Signature. When using the grid, X will be used for the column and Y will be used for the row. The grid plot will be placed where these two intersect. Worksheets that can be used with The Sigil Self are available in the back of this book or for free download at curiohut.com.

For Yourself and Others

You can use The Sigil Self system to uncover your own Cosmic Signature or to help others find theirs. Start with your own grid. Learn how each station builds upon the next, and witness how your Sigil forms a visual and energetic expression of your identity. The insights you gain will deepen your understanding of your path, your gifts and your design.

Once you are familiar with the process, you can create Cosmic Signatures for your friends, loved ones, or clients. Each reading is unique and deeply personal. This system is not just a self-exploration tool, it's also a meaningful activity you can share with others.

Whether you are a seeker, practitioner or simply curious, The Sigil Self gives you a structured, symbolic and intuitive method to map identity through number and form.

How to Calculate Your Numbers

There are example finished worksheets on page 118 for your reference. Take a peek and get a sense of what they look like. You can always reference them again in more detail as you get started in the Walkthrough.

Introduction

Let's learn about calculating the numbers, but don't start yours quite yet. Wait until the walkthrough section.

To journey through the eight stations of The Sigil Self, you will need to translate your name and date of birth into vibrational numbers using the Pythagorean Numerology System. The process is simple yet powerful. Each letter corresponds to a number between 1 and 9, and every number carries with it a symbolic resonance that reflects part of your spiritual frequency.

You will use this method throughout the book to plot coordinates on the 9x9 grid, discover Archetypes and uncover the hidden patterns in your identity.

See Conversion Chart below

1	2	3	4	5	6	7	8	9
A	B	C	D	E	F	G	H	I
J	K	L	M	N	O	P	Q	R
S	T	U	V	W	X	Y	Z	

Name Calculation

On the worksheet, you'll calculate numbers for your first, middle and last name, as well as combinations of them.

Step 1 - Write your name

Step 2 - Match each letter to the corresponding number

Step 3 - Add the numbers together

Step 4 - Reduce the total to a single digit

Example : First Name - LUNA

L = 3

U = 3

N = 5

A = 1

3 + 3 + 5 + 1 = 12

1 + 2 = 3

The First Name Number is 3

This same process is used for First, Middle and Last names

Example: Personality Number - Luna Marie Stone

The Personality Number is all consonants from your whole name. First identify the consonants.

Luna - L, N
Marie - M, R
Stone - S, T, N

Consonant Sequence = L, N, M, R, S, T, N

Next match each consonant to its number

L = 3

N = 5

M = 4

R = 9

S = 1

T = 2

N = 5

Now add all the numbers together

$3 + 5 + 4 + 9 + 1 + 2 + 5 = 29$

Reduce to a single digit

$2 + 9 = 11$

$1 + 1 = 2$

The Personality Number is 2

Example: Soul Number - Luna Marie Stone

The Soul Number is all the vowels from your whole name. First identify all the vowels.

Luna - U, A

Marie - A, I, E

Stone - O, E

Vowel sequence = U, A, A, I, E, O, E

Next match all the vowels to numbers

U = 3

A = 1

A = 1

I = 9

E = 5

O = 6

E = 5

Now add all the numbers together

$3 + 1 + 1 + 9 + 5 + 6 + 5 = 30$

$3 + 0 = 3$

Your Soul Number is 3

Example: **Destiny Number - Luna Marie Stone**

For the Destiny Number every letter from the whole name will be used.

L U N A M A R I E S T O N E

Convert letter to number and add

$3 + 3 + 5 + 1 + 4 + 1 + 9 + 9 + 5 + 1 + 2 + 6 + 5 + 5 = 59$

Reduce to a single digit

$5 + 9 = 14$

$1 + 4 = 5$

Your Destiny Number is 5

Important Note: When calculating Personality, Soul, and Destiny numbers, always start with the core letters of the full name. Do not use the reduced totals from the first, middle, last name calculations you did earlier. Those are used for separate insights and will give an incorrect result if used here.

Date Calculation

Let's say your birthday is June 24th, 1986

Break it into parts

Month (June) = 6

Day (24) = $2 + 4 = 6$

Year (1986) = $1 + 9 + 8 + 6 = 24 (2 + 4) = 6$

Life Path Number

Life path number is calculated using the full birth date (month, day and year)

Add the reduced values together

6 (month) + 6 (day) + 6 (year) = 18

Reduce to a single digit

1 + 8 =9

Your Life Path Number is 9

Important Note: Life Path vs Name Numbers
When calculating Life Path Numbers, you must reduce the month, day and year separately before adding them together.
This is different than how you calculate Personality, Soul and Destiny numbers, where you always begin with the core letters of any name and never use any previously reduced totals.
Following this method keeps your calculations aligned with the system and ensures accurate results.

What You Will Need

- Pen or Pencil
- This Book
- Blank paper
- The Sigil Self Worksheets in the back of book or download free at curiohut.com
- A Calculator
- A quiet space
- A ruler or straightedge

Most of these are optional but recommended to make The Sigil Self easier and more enjoyable to use.

Important Note about Names
Your name carries power. In this system, that includes your chosen name. Whether you go by your birth name, married name, spiritual name or any other name you identify with, The Sigil Self welcomes that choice. Trust your intuition, you know which name carries your truth.

Calculating your X and Y

Each Station will provide you with directions for X and Y coordinates. You will need to reference your reduced numbers from the Numerology and Cosmic Signature worksheet to find your grid coordinates.

Example:
In station 1 X = Last Name Numerology. Reference your worksheet and find your reduced last name result. If your last name was Stone, then your X coordinate will be 1.

In station 1 the Y = Birth Year Numerology. Reference your worksheet and find your reduced birth year number. If your birth year was 1980, then your birth year number will be 9.

The X is for the column and the Y is for the row.

You will write a #1 in the square where X1 and Y9 intersect.

As you progress to other stations you will start drawing the lines of your Sigil connecting 1 to 2, 2 to 3 and so on.

To find your Ancestral Archetype in Station 1 you will calculate X + Y. In our example we had X1 and Y9.

$1 + 9 = 10$
$1 + 0 = 1$

The Ancestral Archetype Number is 1.

The Worksheets

The Cosmic Signature Worksheet:

The Cosmic Signature Worksheet is the main worksheet you will be using during the journey of the Sigil Self. In the center of the worksheet you will see the 9x9 square. At the top of the square is the X axis and to the left of the square you will see the Y axis. Using the X for the columns and Y for the rows, this is where at each Station you will find where your X and Y intersect and find your grid plot. The grid plot will be marked with a number between 1 and 8 depending on which station you are working on. As you progress from station 1 to 2 for example, you will then draw a line connecting 1 to 2 and so forth as you progress to the next stations.

Around the grid are 8 circles. Starting at the 12 o'clock position is Station 1. Moving clockwise around the circle is Station 2 and so on. To the left of each circle is an X, this is where you will write in the X grid co-ordinate. To the right of each circle is a Y where you will write in the Y grid coordinate. Above each circle is a number designating which station it is, and in the top of the circle is the Station name. In the center of the circle you will write in your total of X + Y and below it you will write in your answer. Example Seeker, Receptive, Helm, etc....

At the top left of The Cosmic Signature Worksheet you will see boxes for the birth date reduced totals. You will fill in your reduced total for the Month, Day and Year. Then you will calculate your Life Path Number and fill in that box with the reduced total as well. You can use The Numerology Worksheet to aid in the calculations.

At the top right of The Cosmic Signature Worksheet you will see boxes for the Name Numerology totals. You will fill in the boxes with the reduced totals of your first, middle and last name. You will also fill in the boxes for your Personality Number, Soul Number and Destiny Number. You can use The Numerology Worksheet to aid with the calculations.

In the bottom left of The Cosmic Signature Worksheet you will see a letter to number quick reference chart.

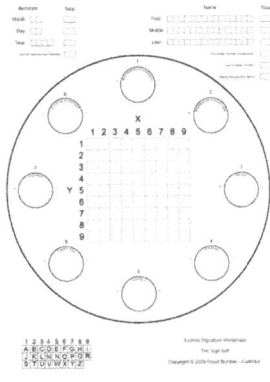

Introduction

The Numerology Worksheet:

The Numerology Worksheet has a large portion that mimics a piece of graph paper. It can be used in place of scratch paper to aid with calculations. There's no right or wrong way to use it, just use as needed. Once the calculations are complete transfer the reduced totals to the Cosmic Signature Worksheet.

In the bottom left corner of The Numerology Worksheet you will see a letter to number quick reference chart.

In the bottom right corner you will see a reminder of the formulas for Life Path Number, Personality Number, Soul Number and Destiny Number.

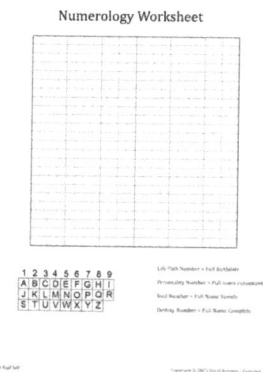

The Cosmic Signature Sheet:

Once you are completed with all 8 Stations and your Cosmic Signature Worksheet is finished you can optionally transfer your Sigil by tracing it to the Cosmic Signature Sheet. This will give you a nice clean Sigil without the 9x9 square, grid and plot numbers. This sheet also has spaces where you can write in your station results in the circles. You can choose to use the Numbers, Names, Sigils or a combination of them. Use whatever feels right.

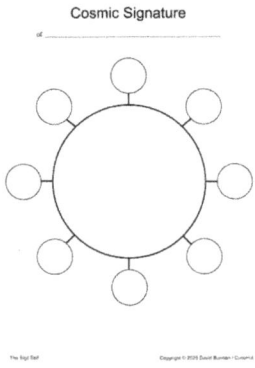

The Sigil of Self Sheet:

Similar to the Cosmic Signature Sheet, this sheet has a place where you can trace your Sigil over and make it nice and clean. This sheet focuses on the Sigil only and does not have spaces for the Station results. Once again this sheet is optional.

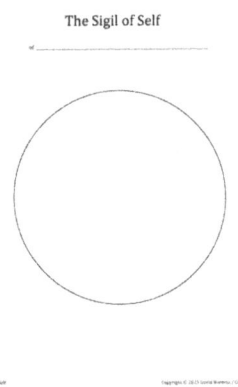

Introduction

Let's Get Ready:

The introduction is complete. Feel free to reference back to it any time you need. Next up is your calculations and beginning The Walkthrough. I hope you enjoy your Journey of the Sigil Self.

WELCOME

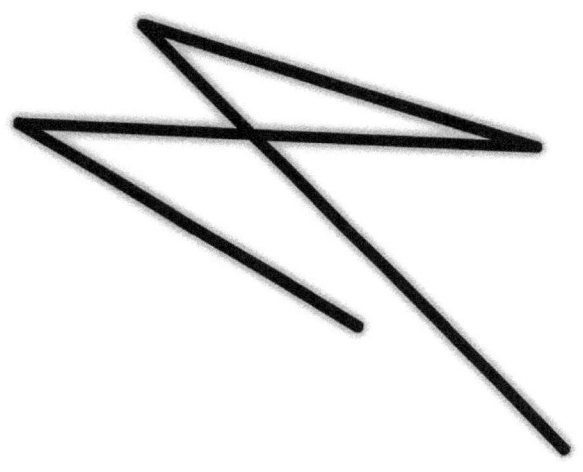

to The Sigil Self

Walkthrough

First calculate your date and name numbers. You can use the worksheets that are available in the back of this book or available for free download at curiohut.com.

Start with the Numerology Worksheet and transfer the reduced totals to the boxes at the top of the Cosmic Signature Worksheet.

When you are ready and all your reduced totals are filled out on the top section of the Cosmic Signature Worksheet move onto station 1

Station 1 - Ancestral Archetype

Your Ancestral Archetype is your origin. It's decoded from your surname and the calendar year you were born. The Ancestral Archetype reflects deep rooted traits and unconscious patterns inherited from your generational energy.

Coordinates:
X = Last Name Numerology
Y = Birth Year Numerology
X + Y = Ancestral Archetype

Find the Station 1 circle located at the north position. Reference your worksheet and find your reduced last name result and write it below the X. Find the reduced birth year result and write it below the Y.

Calculate your X + Y, reduce if needed and write the number inside the station 1 circle.

Reference the Ancestral Archetype list and find yours. Write the name in the lower part of the station 1 circle.

Place a number 1 in the grid square where your X and Y intersect. This is your starting point, no lines are drawn in station1.

Ancestral Archetypes

1 - Seeker
Driven by Curiosity and independence, The seeker ventures out to discover the unknown.

For more information see page 35

2 - Emissary

Walkthrough

A bridge between worlds, The Emissary brings harmony through empathy, diplomacy and subtle influence.

For more information see page 36

3 - Muse
Full of creative spark, The Muse inspires others through artistic expression and emotional presence.

For more information see page 37

4 - Warden
The trustworthy protector, The Warden brings order, structure and reliability to the world.

For more information see page 38

5 - Wanderer
Unbound and ever-changing, The Wanderer follows instinct and experience in pursuit of freedom and growth.

For more information see page 39

6 - Guardian
The comforting nurturer, The Guardian safeguards others through love, care and duty.

For more information see page 40

7 - Weaver
Quiet and perceptive, The Weaver senses the unseen and gains insight from their keen observations.

For more information see page 41

8 - Magnate
Strategic and commanding, The Magnate shapes reality through ambition, power and long term vision.

For more information see page 42

9 - Luminary
An enlightened guide, The Luminary leads with compassion, wisdom and the radiance of life experience.

For more information see page 43

Read more information about your Ancestral Archetype on the reference page.

Move on to Station 2

Walkthrough

Station 2 - Personal Archetype

Your Personal Archetype represents the unevolved version of the self. Partly influenced by ancestry and partially influenced by your upbringing. It's decoded from your Ancestral Archetype and your Day of Birth.

Coordinates:
X = Ancestral Archetype Number
Y = Birthday Numerology (day only)
X + Y = Personal Archetype

Find the Station 2 circle located at the north east position. Reference Station 1 and your Ancestral Archetype Number, write it below the X. Find the reduced birth day result and write it below the Y.

Calculate your X + Y, reduce if needed and write the number inside the station 2 circle.

Reference the Personal Archetype list and find yours. Write the name in the lower part of the station 2 circle.

Place a number 2 in the grid square where your X and Y intersect. Draw your first line of your Cosmic Signature connecting point 1 to point 2.

Personal Archetypes

1 - Seeker
A self-starter with strong inner drive, The Seeker walks their own path with courage and independence.

For more information see page 44

2 - Emissary
Thriving through personal connection, The Emissary is balanced, diplomatic and strives to bring harmony to the world.

For more information see page 45

3 - Muse
Expressive and emotional, The Muse lives through creativity and inspiring others.

For more information see page 46

4 - Warden
Grounded and responsible, The Warden is practical, loyal and dependable.

For more information see page 47

Walkthrough

5 - Wanderer

Trusting their gut, The Wanderer resists routine, chases freedom and yearns for new adventures.

For more information see page 48

6 - Guardian

Protective and heartfelt, The Guardian leads with compassion, choosing care and duty over ego and ambition.

For more information see page 49

7 - Weaver

Perceptive and intuitive, The Weaver senses the unspoken and unseen.

For more information see page 50

8 - Magnate

Ambitious and deliberate, The Magnate knows only success while shaping their destiny.

For more information see page 51

9 - Luminary

Wise beyond their years, The Luminary brings light and meaning to others through insight and empathy.

For more information see page 52

Read more information about your Personal Archetype on the reference page.

Move on to Station 3

Station 3 - Psyche

The station reveals the inner Psyche of how you choose to think, feel and process the world around you. Decoded from your First Name and your Personal Archetype. This Psyche represents the perceptive and emotional tone of the self.

Coordinates:
X = Personal Archetype Number
Y = First Name Numerology
X + Y = Psyche Type

Find the Station 3 circle located at the east position. Reference Station 2 and your Personal Archetype Number, write it below the X. Find the reduced first name result and write it below the Y.

Calculate your X + Y, reduce if needed and write the number inside the station 3 circle.

Reference the Psyche Type list and find yours. Write the name in the lower part of the station 3 circle.

Place a number 3 in the grid square where your X and Y intersect. Continue your Cosmic Signature by drawing a line connecting point 2 to point 3.

Psyche Types

1 - The Initiating
Driven and vision focused, you are quick to take action while others hesitate.

For more information see page 53

2 - The Unifying
Empathetic to others, you bring peace, cooperation and cohesion. You are sensitive to the energy around you and value personal connections.

For more information see page 54

3 - The Visionary
Expressive and imaginative, you express yourself through art, ideas and emotion.

For more information see page 55

4 - The Grounded
Calculating and practical, you seek structure and efficiency. Your patience and discipline are never in short supply.

For more information see page 56

5 - The Unbound
Restless and curious, you are driven by a need to explore, internally and externally. You gather knowledge through trial and error.

For more information see page 57

6 - The Devoted
Protective and loyal, you care deeply, show your strength through service and create emotional safety for others.

For more information see page 58

7 - The Receptive

Spirit Attuned and introspective, you are drawn to the unseen. Through dream, divination and reflection you seek wisdom beyond traditional logic.

For more information see page 59

8 - The Ambitious

Rebellious and disruptive, you break what needs to be broken by confronting hypocrisy and pushing boundaries.

For more information see page 60

9 - The Empathetic

Inspirational and uplifting, you embody purpose, vision and hope.

For more information see page 61

Read more information about your Psyche Type on the reference page .

Move on to Station 4

Station 4 - Persona

Your Persona is the mask you show to the world. It's molded by expectation, adaptation and social roles. It represents the self that navigates external reality, this is not who you entirely are, rather who you let others see. The Persona Type is decoded by your Psyche Type number and the Numerology of your Middle Name.

Coordinates:
X = Psyche Type Number
Y = Middle Name Numerology
X + Y = Persona Type

Find the Station 4 circle located at the south east position. Reference Station 3 and your Psyche Type Number, write it below the X. Find the reduced middle name result and write it below the Y.

Calculate your X + Y, reduce if needed and write the number inside the station 4 circle.

Reference the Persona Type list and find yours. Write the name in the lower part of the station 4 circle.

Place a number 4 in the grid square where your X and Y intersect. Continue your Cosmic Signature by drawing a line connecting point 3 to point 4.

Persona Types

1 - Helm
Worn by those who lead, The Helm is bold, driven and protective.

For more information see page 62

2 - Veil
Soft spoken and enigmatic, The Veil appears composed, intuitive and emotionally attuned.

For more information see page 63

3 - Garland
Adorned with beauty and charm, The Garland expresses joy and flair, a public facing Persona that inspires.

For more information see page 64

4 - Coif
Simple and enduring, The Coif presents as disciplined, reliable and humble.

For more information see page 65

5 - Hood
Unbound and elusive, The Hood is The Persona of quiet defiance and resistance to conformity.

For more information see page 66

6 - Shawl
Warm and inviting, The Shawl is a nurturing Persona, gentle, protective and openly caring.

For more information see page 67

7 - Cowl
Quiet and withdrawn, The Cowl projects mystery, depth and introspection.

For more information see page 68

8 - Crown

A symbol of poise, The Crown projects command, wealth and dignified presence. It's worn by those who lead through status.

For more information see page 69

9 - Halo

Radiant and uplifting The Halo is the outward glow of compassion and moral clarity.

For more information see page 70

Read more information about your Persona Type on the reference page.

Move on to Station 5

Station 5 - Inhibition

This is the internal friction that limits your potential. Shaped from a combination of your Persona Type Number and your Personality Number. Your inhibition reflects your fear, block or wound that must be faced to move forward. It's not a flaw, it's a challenge to your evolution. What holds you back also points to what you are here to overcome.

Coordinates:
X = Persona Type Number
Y = Personality Number
X + Y = Inhibition Type

Find the Station 5 circle located at the south position. Reference Station 4 and your Persona Type Number, write it below the X. Find the Personality Number result and write it below the Y.

Calculate your X + Y, reduce if needed and write the number inside the station 5 circle.

Reference the Inhibition Type list and find yours. Write the name in the lower part of the station 5 circle. Place a number 5 in the grid square where your X and Y intersect. Continue your Cosmic Signature by drawing a line connecting point 4 to point 5.

Inhibition Types

1 - Dependency

Fearful and drained, it's the internal pull to give away your power.

For more information see page 71

2 - Selfishness

Prioritizes yourself above all else, often disrupting balance and connections.

For more information see page 72

3 - Apathy

Lack of inspiration, feels indifferent to beauty, inspiration or creation.

For more information see page 73

4 - Chaos

Unstable, disorganized, resists structure and long term effort.

For more information see page 74

5 - Obligation

Feels bound by duty or expectations, trapped by roles.

For more information see page 75

6 - Neglect

Avoids responsibility, fails to show up for others and for themselves.

For more information see page 76

7 - Shallowness

Avoids depth, evades self reflection, stuck within surface level distractions.

For more information see page 77

8 - Stagnation

Resists change or growth, stuck in the pursuit of comfort or control.

For more information see page 78

9 - Isolation

Withdrawn from others, cut off from purpose, belief or connection.

For more information see page 79

Read more information about your Inhibition Type on the reference page.

Move on to Station 6

Station 6 - Core Virtue

Your core virtue reveals the inner strength that rises to face your inhibition. This station is shaped by your Inhibition Number and your Life Path Number. Your core virtue is not something you are given, it's something that you have developed through hardship and life experiences. Your core virtue is a guiding principle, something you can lean on whenever your path is unclear.

Coordinates:
X = Inhibition Number
Y = Life Path Number
X + Y = Core Virtue Type

Find the Station 6 circle located at the south west position. Reference Station 5 and your Inhibition Type Number, write it below the X. Find the Life Path Number result and write it below the Y.

Calculate your X + Y, reduce if needed and write the number inside the station 6 circle.

Reference the Core Virtue Type list and find yours. Write the name in the lower part of the station 6 circle.

Place a number 6 in the grid square where your X and Y intersect. Continue your Cosmic Signature by drawing a line connecting point 5 to point 6.

Core Virtue Types

1 - Courage
The will to act despite fear, forging forward through the unknown.

For more information see page 80

2 - Compassion
The ability to feel deeply for others while still honoring your own needs.

For more information see page 81

3 - Resilience
The strength to rise after setback, failure or loss.

For more information see page 82

4 - Integrity
Living in alignment with your moral values, even when there is a personal cost.

For more information see page 83

Walkthrough

5 - Wisdom
Insight gained through reflection, pain and observation.

For more information see page 84

6 - Devotion
Unshakable loyalty to the purpose and people that matter to you most.

For more information see page 85

7 - Authenticity
The power to be yourself fully, without apology or mask.

For more information see page 86

8 - Adaptability
The grace to change with life's cycles while holding steady within.

For more information see page 87

9 - Vision
A forward looking clarity that sees beyond the present.

For more information see page 88

Read more information about your Core Virtue Type on the reference page.

Move on to Station 7

Station 7 - Inspiration

This station reveals inspiration cultivated from your Core Virtue Type Number and your Soul Number. It's the voice beneath the surface, the quiet knowing that speaks when the world goes silent. Here you will uncover your personal mantra, a phrase drawn from your learned wisdom and shaped by your journey. Whether said aloud or within, this insight is yours to draw strength from. Use it to strengthen and fortify your Core Virtue.

Coordinates:
X = Core Virtue Number
Y = Soul Number
X + Y = Inspiration

Walkthrough

Find the Station 7 circle located at the west position. Reference Station 6 and your Core Virtue Type Number, write it below the X. Find the Soul Number result and write it below the Y.

Calculate your X + Y, reduce if needed and write the number inside the station 7 circle.

Reference the Inspiration Type list and find yours. Write the name in the lower part of the station 7 circle.

Place a number 7 in the grid square where your X and Y intersect. Continue your Cosmic Signature by drawing a line connecting point 6 to point 7.

Inspiration Types

1 - Renewal
"I am the one who begins again"

For more information see page 89

2 - Unity
"I am part of a greater whole"

For more information see page 90

3 - Joy
"My joy is sacred"

For more information see page 91

4 - Sincerity
"What I build reflects who I am"

For more information see page 92

5 - Change
"Change is my ally, not my enemy"

For more information see page 93

6 - Love
"Love is the root of my strength"

For more information see page 94

7 - Reflection
"Stillness holds answers"

For more information see page 95

8 - Resilience
"I adapt, but I do not vanish"

For more information see page 96

9 - Radiance
"My light shines on those around me"

For more information see page 97

Read more information about your Inspiration on the reference page.

Move on to Station 8

Station 8 - Evolved Archetype

This final Station shows who you are becoming, formed from your Inspiration Phrase Number and your Destiny Number. It represents your potential, an Archetype not inherited or chosen but earned through the integration of all other Stations. This is the culmination of your path, the version of the self forged by effort, insight and transformation. The Evolved Archetype shows how your Cosmic Signature radiates when fully embodied, aligned and awake.

Coordinates:
X = Inspiration Phrase Number
Y = Destiny Number
X + Y = Evolved Archetype

Find the Station 8 circle located at the north west position. Reference Station 7 and your Inspiration Type Number, write it below the X. Find the Destiny Number result and write it below the Y.

Calculate your X + Y, reduce if needed and write the number inside the station 8 circle.

Reference the Evolved Archetype Type list and find yours. Write the name in the lower part of the station 8 circle.

Place a number 8 in the grid square where your X and Y intersect. Finish your Cosmic Signature by drawing a line connecting point 7 to point 8.

Evolved Archetypes

Walkthrough

1 - Seeker

You have become the one who never stops growing, always in pursuit of truth, freedom and the next adventure. Evolution is your fuel.

For more information see page 98

2 - Emissary

You have become a bridge between worlds, you embody grace, empathy and the sacred art of connection. You unify what others divide.

For more information see page 99

3 - Muse

You have become a vessel for beauty and meaning, infusing the world with color, story and emotion. Your presence evokes feeling in those around you.

For more information see page 100

4 - Warden

You have become the steward of order, building systems, protecting what matters and holding strong under pressure.

For more information see page 101

5 - Wanderer

You have become the spark that breaks cycles, one who can change the landscape by simply moving through them. Restlessness becomes revolution.

For more information see page 102

6 - Guardian

You have become love in motion, anchored by compassion, and lifted by duty. You nurture transformation in those around you.

For more information see page 103

7 - Weaver

You have become the connection between the seen and unseen, the one who understands truth not by sight, but by resonance.

For more information see page 104

8 - Magnate
You have become the architect of success, wielding power with vision on purpose. You do not seek influence, you attract it.

For more information see page 105

9 - Luminary
You have become a light for others to follow, you emanate clarity, compassion and wisdom.

For more information see page 106

Read more information about your Evolved Archetype on the reference page.

Your Cosmic Signature is complete, see Your Cosmic Signature section on page 110 to learn about next steps.

Congratulations

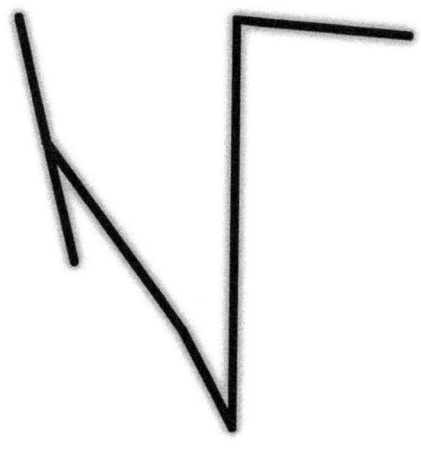

Walkthrough

Reference

1 - The Seeker

You descend from a restless lineage. The Seekers are those who broke way from outdated traditions in pursuit of something more meaningful. The Seekers bloodline is one of departure not destination. Whether physically, spiritually or ideologically the Seekers before you refused to settle for the life that was handed to them.

This Archetype imprints with a yearning to move, question and carve your own path, but it also carries the burden of disconnection. You may feel cut off from your roots, unsure of where "home" really is, or why staying still gives you the feeling of surrender. The legacy you hold is one of courage and defiance, but also exile. What was passed down to you is not a map, but the desire to make one.

Your karmic roots may include family systems fractured by distance or beliefs. You were handed the echo of movement, and the task of deciding whether or not to continue the search or finally arrive at your destination.

Inherited Patterns:
- A tendency to seek meaning though change or movement
- Discomfort with tradition, routine or expected roles
- A legacy of non-conformity and pioneering spirit

Transformational Potential:
You have the opportunity to break the cycle of restlessness, not by abandoning the Seeker's drive, but by refining the purpose. You may be the one who finally turns the journey into a home, or a question into a creed.

Seeker

Reference: Station 1 - Ancestral Archetypes

2 - The Emissary

You come from a line of intermediaries, those who stood at the crossroads between people, ideas or opposing forces. Your ancestral echo is one of diplomacy, harmony and the quiet strength of those who kept the peace while remaining in the shadows. These were the gentle balancers such as mediators, caretakers and message bearers passing between generations, cultures and beliefs.

The Emissary as an inherited archetype suggests your roots are woven from compromise and cohesion. Your lineage placed great value on unity and emotional intelligence. They would not hesitate to sacrifice for the sake of others. You may have been raised in an environment where keeping the peace was prized above all else and where emotional awareness was expected.

This ancestral energy gives you an uncanny ability to read a room, leaves you finely attuned to tension and equipped with the tools to soften it, but it may also leave you prone to self suppression.

Inherited Patterns:
- A family legacy of care-taking or middle child dynamics
- Generational pressure to be the glue that holds others together
- A learned skill of negotiation or people pleasing

Transformational Potential:
You carry the opportunity to redefine what it means to harmonize. Your role is not to erase yourself for the sake of peace, but to hold the space where truth and cohesion exist as one. You are here to stitch them together in a way that honors every thread, including your own.

Emissary

Reference: Station 1 - Ancestral Archetypes

3 - The Muse

You come from a line of creators, performers and visionaries, those who found beauty in chaos and drew meaning from the depths of emotion. The Muse appears in your ancestral line as a reminder that life is not meant to be lived muted. Your lineage carries the spark of storytellers, artists and emotionally expressive souls who shape reality though the lens of imagination.

This inherited imprint suggests that creativity was not just admired in your line, it was essential. Perhaps your ancestors used humor, performance and poetic truth as a way to cope, connect or carve out a space in the world that demanded that they conform. Their legacy pulses through you as emotional intensity, a magnetic presence and an urge to transform pain into art.

With this gift also comes an inherited struggle because emotional sensitivity runs deep. You may carry the ancestral wounds of being misunderstood, dismissed or silenced. The Muse Archetype is not always met with applause, it often comes from the need to speak when no one is listening.

Inherited Patterns:
- Emotional expressiveness passed down through art, performance or mood
- A legacy of charm, sensitivity and emotional unpredictability
- The burden of being "the light" or entertainer in difficult circumstances

Transformational Potential:
You have inherited a flame that longs to dance. You are not here to be swept away by emotional tides, you are here to shape them. The Muse in your bloodline is not merely about beauty, it's about alchemy. You carry that alchemy forward to inspire, provoke and to move the world by being emotionally alive.

Muse

Reference: Station 1 - Ancestral Archetypes

4 - The Warden

You descend from a lineage forged in duty and protection, those who held the line when others faltered. The Warden appears as a stabilizing force in your ancestry, a legacy of guardianship passed down through generations. These were the foundation layers, rule keepers and the ones who bore the weight of responsibility so the bloodline would not break.

The Archetype suggests that your family line carried a deep reverence for responsibility, perseverance and clear boundaries. Whether shaped by tradition, discipline or an unshakable moral conduct, your ancestors upheld order over chaos and found strength in consistency. Their stability was hard earned, built through sacrifice, long hours and emotional suppression for the sake of others.

You have inherited this archetype not just as a blueprint for protection, but as a reminder that the structures you build become the shelter for those who follow.

Inherited Patterns:
- Generational influence of discipline and rules
- Unspoken pressure to be a provider
- Legacy of emotional containment in service of greater responsibility

Transformational Potential:
Your roots have been fortified with intention, brick by brick, vow by vow. You are not bound to repeat these patterns unchanged. Your task is not to break the wall down, but to find the door and walk through it. You inherit the strength to build but you also have the strength to evolve, you are the bridge between legacy and change, structure and soul.

Warden

Reference: Station 1 - Ancestral Archetypes

5 - The Wanderer

You come from a legacy of rebels, drifters and untamed spirits, those who defied convention not necessarily to make a statement but because it's their nature. The Wanderer appears revealing a history shaped by movement, adaptability and a refusal to be tethered.

Whether physically nomadic or emotionally elusive, your ancestors may have lived outside the lines of what society calls acceptable. They switch roles, places and identities with ease, following seasons, whims or inner callings. The Wanderer is always seeking something just beyond their reach. Some may have been considered misfits, explorers and exiles, others simply could not stay where they were expected to.

This inheritance has gifted you a wild heart and keen instincts of survival. But it may also come with the burden of disconnection, restlessness and avoidance. There is great strength in your blood, but it does not settle easily.

Inherited Patterns:
- Generational avoidance or staying still, routines and commitments
- A legacy of adaptation, invention and departure
- Difficulty forming deep roots and developing trust

Transformational Potential:
You carry the gift of freedom, but now it's your choice to decide how to wield it. You can turn inherited drift into conscious exploration. You can move with awareness instead of escape. The Wanderer in your bloodline reminds you that your path was never meant to be paved, it was meant to be discovered. But discovery begins with knowing what you are running towards, not what you are running from.

Wanderer

Reference: Station 1 - Ancestral Archetypes

6 - The Guardian

You come from a line of protectors, caretakers and healers. Silent sentinels who placed the wellbeing of others above their own. Inheriting the Guardian suggests that your roots are steeped in service, loyalty and emotional labor. This lineage has passed down the deep belief that love is best shown through action, and that safety is a responsibility, not a given.

Your ancestors may have sacrificed without complaint. They held the emotional weight of families and communities, in some cases this duty was noble, in others it may have been a burden masked by virtue.

This imprint shaped you with a heightened sensitivity to the needs of others, and perhaps an unconscious script that your own worth is tied to how much you can give or endure. It's a powerful inheritance, but one that requires you to set boundaries to stay in balance.

Inherited Patterns:
- Generational over-responsibility and sacrifice
- Deep loyalty that can blur the line into self neglect
- A protective instinct passed down as identity

Transformational Potential:
You have inherited a heart that knows how to hold space, but be careful because you are not meant to hold the whole world. The Guardian lineage offers you the strength to nurture without depletion and to love without losing yourself. Your evolution begins when you learn that protection does not always mean control, and that you too are worthy of rest.

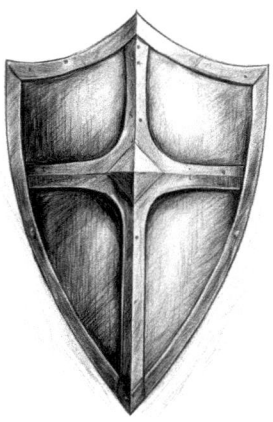

Guardian

Reference: Station 1 - Ancestral Archetypes

7 - The Weaver

You come from a line of silent observers, mystics and spiritual seekers who live more in the internal world than the outer. The Weaver appears as your ancestral imprint suggesting that your roots are tied to deep introspection, symbolic thinking and a search for hidden meaning.

This lineage may have included spiritual practitioners, dreamers, philosophers or simply those who felt different and turned inward for insight rather than outward. Silence may have been survival, secrets may have been protection, but always with a thread connecting the seen to the unseen.

As a descendant of Weavers you inherit the extraordinary ability to see what lies beneath the surface. You may feel a pull to explore memory, mysticism or the unconscious patterns that others overlook. This insight can feel both like a gift and a weight especially if past generations were misunderstood or isolated.

Inherited Patterns:
- Generational secrecy or spiritual gifts passed down silently
- Tendency toward withdrawal and introspection
- A deep hunger for understanding the unknown

Transformational Potential:
You were born with the instinct to connect invisible threads. Yet ancestral gifts require grounding. Your inheritance offers more than solitude, it offers a sacred way of seeing. When you integrate the wisdom of your lineage with the clarity of your own voice, you step into the role of storyteller, pattern keeper and a healer moving across time.

Weaver

Reference: Station 1 - Ancestral Archetypes

8 - The Magnate

You come from a line of builders, those who understood power, strategy and the long game. The Magnate as your ancestral imprint speaks to a legacy of ambition and discipline. Whether your ancestors were land-owners, merchants or leaders, they shaped the world around them through vision and force of will.

This lineage emphasizes legacy, success and reputation. Strength was a currency and control may have been a means for survival. You may carry the gifts of this heritage such as a sharp mind and a commanding presence, but you also carry the burden of a deep pressure to perform.

As a descendant of Magnates, your roots are tied to structures of power, wealth and authority. You have inherited the instinct to lead or manage, even if you would rather not. You may feel an unconscious drive to build or protect something that outlasts you.

Inherited Patterns:
- Pressure to uphold a family name
- Tendency to equate success with financial worth
- Strong desire to organize and control

Transformational Potential:
Your inheritance arrives in the form of blueprints and the tools to forge your own foundation. The work is not to reject your lineage, but to discern which parts of it benefit your soul, and learn what need to be dismantled. When the Magnate energy is awakened, creation becomes devotion and what you build carries intention.

Magnate

Reference: Station 1 - Ancestral Archetypes

9 - Luminary

You come from a line of visionaries, mystics and wisdom keepers, those who held light in dark times, whether seen or unseen. The Luminary as your Ancestral Archetype indicates a lineage rich with inner knowing, moral clarity and spiritual endurance. Your roots may be entwined with service, sacrifice or teachings that were passed down in whispers.

This inheritance can come with both profound grace and silent burdens. Perhaps your ancestors had insight they were not able to express, perhaps they lived for others dimming their own glow in the process. You may carry the echo of that restraint which comes alongside a powerful calling to uplift and to heal from the shadows.

There may be an ancestral pattern here of hiding one's gifts or suppressing spiritual truths. But there is also a legacy of wisdom passed down from generation to generation, even if never spoken aloud.

Inherited Patterns:
- Empathy passed down as both strength and weight
- Tendency to be the unseen support system for others
- A calling to serve or guide, even without acknowledgment

Transformational Potential:
Your inheritance is like a candle, at times it may have been flickering or dim, but it has never gone out. To walk the legacy of the luminary is to remember that your insight is part of your lineage, and your presence is a continuation of light that has been quietly shaping lives for generations. Your path is to honor what came before you, and shine in your own way.

Luminary

Reference: Station 1 - Ancestral Archetypes

1 - The Seeker

The Seeker is the personal path you follow by choice. As your personal Archetype it reveals your inner compass which is restless, instinctive and unwilling to settle. You feel most alive when moving toward something unknown, whether it's a new idea, a creative pursuit or a life change.

You don't just desire change, you embody it. The Seeker shows up in the way you challenge norms, break routines and insist on living with authenticity. You are driven not by the destination, but by the motion itself. What others might consider risky, you call necessary.

This Archetype fuels your will to grow, even if the growth means walking alone. At your best, you are a trailblazer who inspires others simply by your resistance to conform. At your worst, you may disappear into perpetual motion, confusing action with purpose. Each time you choose a path unexpected of you, it affirms the power of your own becoming.

Embodied Traits:
- A hunger for freedom and expansion
- Willingness to endure discomfort to discover truth
- Deep resistance to restriction, routine and stagnation

Power Source
Your will is made of movement. When you listen to your inner restlessness, you will find your way forward. You may not always know where you are headed, but your intuition will always let you know when you are off course. That instinct is one of your greatest strengths and can be trusted.

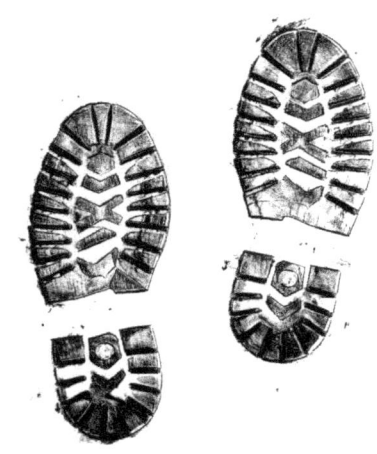

Seeker

Reference: Station 2 - Personal Archetypes

2 - The Emissary

To embody The Emissary is to carry the will of harmony into a divided world. Your instinct leans toward connection and understanding, not control or dominance. As your personal Archetype, The Emissary reveals your strength in presence. You are the one who can hold contradictions without collapsing, speak truths others can't find the words for, and create bridges where there was once walls.

Your personal will expresses through diplomacy, subtle influence and emotional intelligence. You don't need to raise your voice to be heard. Your calm center holds power because it doesn't need to win, it needs to unify. You make people around you feel safe, secure and softened.

When misaligned your voice may dim when trying to maintain the peace. You may avoid conflict out of fear of disruption, or bend too far trying to please everyone. When aligned you are a living channel for healing dialogue, clarity and grace.

Embodied Traits:
- Emotional fluency and inner stillness
- The instinct to meditate, mend and translate
- Deep intuition for timing and tone when communicating

Power Source
Your will is relational. You know the path ahead is not a straight line. You thrive when you listen deeply, speak clearly and reflect upon your inner truth. This is how you shift situations, relationships and even realities.

Emissary

Reference: Station 2 - Personal Archetypes

3 - The Muse

To embody The Muse is to move through life as a spark, igniting emotion, awakening inspiration and revealing possibility in those you touch. Your will is playful, expressive and magnetic. You're not here to repeat what has already been said. You are here to re-imagine it into something vivid and alive.

Your personal power lies in your ability to express what others can't. Through art, words, humor or simply the way you live, you carry an energy that lifts and stirs. When aligned you are a conduit for beauty, spontaneity and emotional truth. People don't just admire you, they feel awakened by you.

In misalignment, you may seek validation through performance or lose direction chasing constant stimulation. You resist structure and commitment out of fear it will cage your creativity. When you are able to center your will on authentic expression you become a living source of inspiration, joyful, raw and real.

Embodied Traits:
- Spontaneity and emotional openness
- The drive to create, share and enchant
- Sensitivity to beauty, humor and rhythm

Power Source
Your will emerges in moments of pure expression, when you stop censoring yourself and start channeling your truth. You don't need to explain yourself to others, just live your authentic life and show others how alive they could feel.

Muse

4 - The Warden

To embrace The Warden is to move through life with intention and structure. Your will is not measured by how fast you move, but by how deeply you commit. You are the anchor others cling to when things are feeling unstable. Your strength is not loud, but it's undeniable.

Your will emerges through consistency. You show up, hold the line and build what lasts. Whether you are protecting what matters or creating things that support others, your presence gives shape to the formless. You carry the blueprint of order in a chaotic world.

In misalignment The Warden may become rigid, controlling and resistant to change. Fear of disorder can lead to overcorrection or emotional detachment. When your actions are rooted in values and not fear, you can create sanctuaries where growth is possible because the ground beneath it is strong.

Embodied Traits:
- Steadfast commitment and quiet authority
- Integrity driven action and moral responsibility
- Inner calm that stabilizes those around you

Power Source
Your power comes from being the structure for others to lean on, but it begins by building that very structure within yourself. When you live by your own well formed values, your very presence will become an act of service.

Warden

Reference: Station 2 - Personal Archetypes

5 - The Wanderer

The Wanderer represents living by intuition, adaptation and inner navigation. Your will is untamed, you don't just resist the confines of convention, you dissolve them as you go. You move not because you are lost but because you are following an invisible compass that only you can feel.

You're not here to plant a flag or follow a map. You are here to respond to life as it unfolds in front of you and welcome new experiences without forcing outcomes. Know and remember that your identity is forged in flexibility. As you walk your path trust that whatever you need you will find along the way, as long as you keep going.

In misalignment The Wanderer may drift too far and become ungrounded, noncommittal or evasive. When aligned your journey gains meaning. You become the one who moves through the unknown with grace. You have the gift to show others how to let go of certainty and still find their way.

Embodied Traits:
- Deep sensitivity to change and subtle shifts
- Natural improvisation in unfamiliar environments
- Willingness to explore without the need to arrive

Power Source
Your strength isn't in roots, it's in rhythm. When you stop trying to define yourself and instead follow the pulse of your inner freedom your path becomes sacred. You don't escape, you evolve.

Wanderer

Reference: Station 2 - Personal Archetypes

6 - The Guardian

To walk the path of The Guardian is to embrace loyalty, care and commitment. Your will is expressed through service as you protect, lend and support not as an obligation, but because your strength thrives in devotion.

You are someone who anchors others. Your identity doesn't stop with you alone, it branches out to those you nurture and defend. This is no weakness, it's a sacred responsibility. You guard emotional ground, offer unseen labor and carry burdens most people don't notice but rely on.

In misalignment Guardians may lose themselves in caretaking and become resentful. When in alignment your compassion becomes your power. You become the protector your loved ones can count on.

Embodied Traits:
- Fierce devotion to people, principles and service
- Deep emotional endurance and reliability
- A calling to protect, stabilize and heal

Power Source
Your strength comes from the heart through action. When you step into your role as protector and supporter you become the hearth others gather around. You don't just hold space, you create sanctuary.

Guardian

Reference: Station 2 - Personal Archetypes

7 - The Weaver

The Weaver moves through life using intuition, making connections and making time for self reflection. As a Weaver you don't act impulsively, you feel your way forward, sensing patterns and trends where others only see noise. Your will reveals itself not through force, but through synthesis. You bring cohesion to complexity. You listen deeply and act from an inner knowing.

You are pushed by a desire to understand what lies beneath the surface. This curiosity comes in many forms such as introspection, spiritual study or emotional insight. Your power lives in the unseen and you are able to shape meaning through fragments as you connect the dots others overlook. The Weaver is capable of making the invisible visible.

When out of alignment you may spiral into overthinking and withdraw becoming trapped in a web of your own mind. When you trust your inner vision you become a force for revelation and healing.

Embodied Traits:
- Deeply intuitive and fluent in understanding symbology
- Drawn to uncover hidden truths
- Processes through reflection, solitude and ritual

Power Source
Your will is woven not hammered. When you lean into your natural ability of perception you become a keeper of wisdom. You are not here to dominate, you are here to decode mystery.

Weaver

Reference: Station 2 - Personal Archetypes

8 - The Magnate

To be The Magnate is to lead boldly, with purpose and precision. Your visions are manifested by your strategy and willpower. Your move with authority because you know what it takes to build something that lasts. You act with directness and resolve.

You are compelled to organize chaos into order. You are often seen as commanding, but never careless. You carry the burden of responsibility with pride. You don't just dream of success, you make it, and in doing so you also uplift others.

When out of alignment your will can become rigid, overly dominant and obsessed with micromanaging. When balanced your influence brings stability and empowerment to everyone around you.

Embodied Traits:
- Strategic, structured and grounded in reality
- Naturally authoritative, seen as a leader by others
- Motivated by long term vision and leaving a legacy behind

Power Source
Your strength lies in your ability to organize your ambitions into actions. You are a builder and a shaper of reality. When you act from your deepest values you don't just lead, you elevate.

Magnate

9 - The Luminary

To walk with quiet strength and radiant clarity is the path of The Luminary. Your presence moves through the world like a guiding light offering perspective, wisdom and compassion to those around you. Where others seek to prove, you seek to understand.

As a Luminary you carry with you a deep well of insight that draws from your life experiences, spiritual maturity and empathy. You don't act impulsively. You take the time to consider and make meaningful choices. You lead by example and often hold opinions ahead of your time.

When misaligned you may hesitate to act or withdraw from the world's chaos. When centered your presence alone can inspire change and rally others to be their best versions of themselves.

Embodied Traits:
- Calm, wise and deeply principled
- Guided by compassion for others
- Willing to stand alone if necessary to uphold integrity

Power Source

Your strength lies in your ability to shine without needing attention. Standing tall to represent your values influences others, changing lives by just being your true self.

Luminary

Reference: Station 2 - Personal Archetypes

1 - The Initiating

This Psyche speaks to your inner drive and determination. You welcome new challenges that can be overcome with your fresh ideas. As a self-starter, you are someone who doesn't wait for permission and never backs down from the unknown. Your Psyche is wired to spark change, ignite feelings and lead with instinct. This does not mean that you are always right, but you are never idle.

When out of alignment, this Psyche becomes restless. You may put yourself into situations unprepared and burn bridges for the sake of momentum. Your tendency to lead can warp into domination and your gift of ignition may start fires you didn't intend.

When in alignment, The Initiating Psyche is courageous and catalytic. Your are the one who is first to get the ball rolling and the one who is willing to say the things other won't. You light the fire for others to follow and that's your gift to the world.

Challenges:
- Slowing down to reflect
- Recognizing when to collaborate
- Knowing the difference between impulse and intuition

Gifts:
- Fearless momentum
- Instinctive leadership
- The power to shift stuck energy

Initiating

Reference: Station 3 - Psyche

2 - The Unifying

Unifiers thrive on connection. They use their instinct while interacting and looking for common ground, always trying to build bridges rather than walls. With their natural sense for emotional tone they are able to adjust and soothe to preserve flow. Their strength is in subtle power and deescalation. They can sense tension and find graceful ways to smooth it out.

When misaligned, The Unifier may suppress their own needs for the cause of keeping the peace. They can become over-accommodating and fearful of rejection. Conflict avoidance becomes their trap and they risk losing themselves by bending too far to support others.

In alignment, The Unifier sets clear boundaries while remaining heart centered. They are able to cultivate a mutual understanding without sacrificing their personal truth. A Unifier's presence can calm an entire room of people. With their clear and calm words they can alleviate confusion. Through diplomacy they can help others coexist without compromising integrity.

Challenges:
- Speaking up even when uncomfortable
- Navigating tension without self-sacrifice
- Accepting that not all conflict is bad

Gifts:
- Deep empathy
- Relationship alchemy
- Ability to bring order to emotional chaos

Unifying

Reference: Station 3 - Psyche

3 - The Visionary

The Visionary dwells in a place between the now and the next. They perceive potential in everything and everyone they interact with. They feel compelled to shape unseen possibilities in whatever situation they find themselves. Visionaries are dreamers and inventors, the ones who doodle in the margins and stay up late figuring out solutions to problems. Their mind is a canvas for the future and their gift is planting the seed of change.

In misalignment, The Visionary can drift into fantasy and become frustrated when things don't go the way they were planning. They may struggle to follow through on an idea or feel misunderstood when working in an environment that expects conformity. When their brilliance is unchecked it can scatter leading to overwhelm and self-doubt.

When in alignment, The Visionary learns how to turn their ideas into action. They communicate clearly and have a keen sense for finding good collaborators. Their imagination becomes a tool of transformation and they lead others into new possibilities by believing.

Challenges:
- Balancing inspiration vs execution
- Communicating their abstract ideas
- Staying in the present

Gifts:
- Creative foresight
- Big picture thinking
- Innovation that uplifts others

Visionary

Reference: Station 3 - Psyche

4 - The Grounded

This Psyche embodies an inner calm, offering stability in a chaotic world. These individuals are centered, consistent and unshaken by uncertainty. They don't seek attention, but they are the ones others lean on in times of need. They process life through the senses, value patience and rely on the tangible.

In misalignment, The Grounded can become overly cautious, rigid and resistant to change. They may confuse safety with stagnation or use routine as a shield. Their strong desire for peace can turn into avoidance and their reliability into shambles.

When aligned, The Grounded is a great stabilizer, one who instinctively knows when to stand still and when to move with purpose. They listen deeply and act deliberately to show others that power doesn't have to be loud. Their presence comes from life experience and that experience is their medicine.

Challenges:
- Letting go of control
- Remaining flexible in transition
- Trusting that change will be ok

Gifts:
- Calm resilience
- Sensory awareness
- Dependable follow-through

Grounded

Reference: Station 3 - Psyche

5 - The Unbound

The Unbound Psyche craves adventure without fences. They live for freedom of thought, movement and being. The Unbound recoil from anything that feels limiting or expected. They seek the unknown and always wonder what the next adventure will be. The Unbound tend to be innovators, travelers and non-conformists. The Unbound are mesmerized by endless possibilities.

In misalignment, The Unbound becomes avoidant, reckless and directionless. They may chase freedom at all costs while burning bridges along the way. Restlessness becomes their master, not their compass.

In alignment, they can expand the limits of what was thought possible. They can show others how to live large without apology. They trust the unknown honoring their wild nature and forge new paths with grace. Their life becomes a map for others who also yearn to break free.

Challenges:
- Finishing what they start
- Building trust with others
- Choosing freedom while avoiding destruction

Gifts:
- Limitless perspective
- Daring originality
- Fierce authenticity

Unbound

Reference: Station 3 - Psyche

6 - The Devoted

The Devoted Psyche is built around care that is deep and unwavering. Their sense of purpose is intertwined with loyalty to people and beliefs. Devotion is not passive for them, it's an active enduring expression of love. The Devoted are the ones who stay, support and protect by nurturing others and standing by their vision. The Devoted Psyche plunges in heart first in everything they do.

In misalignment, this Psyche may lose themselves in service. They can become codependent or even martyr-like. Their desire to help may even take precedence over their own needs, leading to burnout and resentment.

When aligned, this Psyche holds power in their resilience. They care deeply and their loving arms become a sanctuary for others.

Challenges:
- Prioritizing their own needs
- Letting go of unhealthy relationships
- Knowing when it is time to walk away

Gifts:
- Unwavering commitment
- Emotional endurance
- Healing presence

Devoted

Reference: Station 3 - Psyche

7 - The Receptive

This Psyche lives in deep alignment with intuition and flow. Instead of charging forward they pause, listen, observe and wait for things to unfold. By no means is this weakness, it's their expression of wisdom. The strength of The Receptive lies in their ability to yield, absorb and adapt. The Receptive Psyche trusts cycles, reads energy and often knows things before they happen.

In misalignment, this Psyche may become overly passive and easily influenced. By avoiding conflict and concrete decision-making they open themselves up to be pushed aside by stronger wills. Fear of disapproval can mute their voice.

When aligned, this Psyche becomes a temple for silent wisdom. They create a safe space for truth to emerge by embracing their highly intuitive skills and calming presence.

Challenges:
- Setting boundaries
- Speaking up when needed
- Trusting their own inner knowing

Gifts:
- Deep intuition
- Emotional comfortability
- Adaptive wisdom

Receptive

Reference: Station 3 - Psyche

8 - The Ambitious

The Ambitious Psyche is all about purpose and results. They don't daydream about what could be, they put their ideas into action. The Ambitious stay committed to long-terms goals with laser focus. This lets their skill set of finding resources, navigating through challenges and executing plans stand out. The Ambitious has a special power to not only see the goal, but also see the path to it.

In misalignment, The Ambitious can come off as domineering or impatient. In the pursuit of their goals they risk burnout, and their need to achieve can eclipse their need to connect with others.

In alignment, their drive is channeled through integrity and as they achieve their goals and rise, they uplift others with them. This Psyche understands that power without a purpose is a hollow existence.

Challenges:
- Slowing down
- Delegating and trusting
- Measuring success beyond metrics

Gifts:
- Strategic thinking
- Relentless drive
- Visionary execution

Ambitious

Reference: Station 3 - Psyche

60

9 - The Empathetic

The Empathetic Psyche is a sacred vessel of emotional understanding. They are sensitive to the unseen and are highly attuned to the energy and emotional state of others. This Psyche is compassionate, sympathetic, and gentle.

When out of alignment, the Empathetic may become overwhelmed easily. They run the risk of losing themselves in the emotional noise around them.

In alignment, The Empathetic Psyche is a beacon of love. They provide support intuitively by using their senses.

Challenges:
- Setting emotional boundaries
- Differentiating between the self and others
- Avoiding emotional burnout

Gifts:
- Deep compassion
- Emotional wisdom
- Healing presence

Empathetic

Reference: Station 3 - Psyche

1 - Helm

Helm is the Persona of leadership. You come across as confident, capable and in control. Others naturally defer to you as they are drawn to your strength. Your presence carries weight and people usually assume you are the one in charge.

This Persona forms in those who equate safety with control. The Helm keeps them steadily moving forward in life and offers protection not just for you but for others as well. The armor of the Helm makes your decisions certain, and others will trust you because they can see that you trust yourself.

Out of alignment, the Helm can harden into a domineering presence. You may push past your limits and ignore input from others because you think it will make you look weak. Others may begin to see you as overbearing and distant. This mask tends to tighten when you are afraid to admit you are overwhelmed.

When the Helm is worn in balance you lead with your presence. You don't act like a know-it-all, and are patient enough to let things unfold. Your strength becomes an anchor, not a shield and people will feel grounded around you. You become a confident force that invites trust rather than demanding it.

Helm

Reference: Station 4 - Persona

2 - Veil

The Veil flows with silent grace, present but unobtrusive, expressive yet elusive. In wearing this mask you are often seen as calm and composed. This is true but there is always something held back. You filter your world by revealing just enough.

This Persona forms when you learn to keep the peace by adapting. The Veil is not about deception, it's about preservation. The Veil allows you to sense tension and soften it, to withhold information but not lie. You navigate through social dynamics by reading the room, adapting and avoiding confrontation. This is a Persona of emotional preservation.

When out of alignment, The Veil Persona can cause you to become overly passive. Preventing the discomfort of others becomes more important than the discomfort of your own. When The Veil is used to avoid all conflict it tends to isolate more than it protects.

When aligned, The Veil is both elegant and wise. Your presence is calm and your actions are honest and intentional. The Veil's restraint will be perceived by others as grace, not distance and you will be the master of your own privacy by choosing what to reveal and when.

Veil

Reference: Station 4 - Persona

3 - The Garland

The Garland is The Persona of charm. It's playful, magnetic and expressive. Your presence alone will light up a room. You are colorful, inviting and unforgettable, and for these reasons people tend to gravitate towards you when they need connection.

This Persona takes shape when you learn to share joy. The Garland doesn't hide who you are, it amplifies the emotional parts of you that connect. When wearing this Persona you lead with charm, openness and creativity, disarming tension through warmth and shared delight.

Out of alignment, this Persona will stop feeling genuine and feel more like a performance. Pain will become hidden under a smile, and your bright exterior becomes your shield.

In alignment, The Garland is a celebration of life. You share light without dimming your own. You are able to connect authentically through effortless shared joy and you don't feel pressured to dazzle. Your power is inspiring others that beauty and wonder are always possible.

Garland

Reference: Station 4 - Persona

4 - The Coif

Composed and dependable, The Coif is the Persona of quiet command. Your presence brings reliability and structure. People instinctively know that they can rely on you. As you calmly navigate chaos with a plan, people will describe you as the core who holds things together.

The Coif Persona forms though discipline and intention. Your life experience has taught you that showing up consistently earns trust, so that's exactly what you do. The Coif Mask leads by example, values precision and moves through life with care. You feel responsible to be the one who keeps things together and running smoothly.

When in misalignment, The Coif can become rigid and distant. You will hide behind your routines and suppress your own needs. You will strive to maintain composure at all costs, even when you need help or rest.

When this Persona is aligned, it offers stability without stiffness. You show up with integrity and create grounded spaces for others while also honoring your own limits. The one who wears The Coif is reliable and intentional to the core.

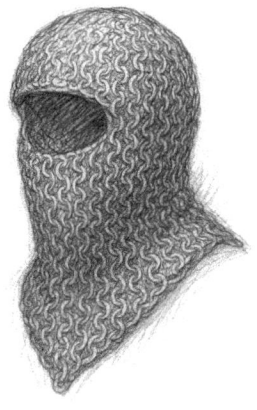

Coif

Reference: Station 4 - Persona

5 - The Hood

The Hood is the Persona of quiet mystery, a presence that people can better feel than explain. People can sense a deep ocean behind your eyes, but they will rarely gain full access. Your surface offers curiosity but provides few answers.

The Hood Persona takes shape when you feel the need to protect your sacred space. It lets you move through life without fully being seen, this is by choice not avoidance. This mask keeps the world away at just the right distance while still remaining within grasp.

In misalignment, The Hood Persona can retreat too far and completely shut others out. You can easily become misunderstood and cause increased distance where there could have been trust.

In alignment, The Hood becomes a selective keeper of the unseen. You engage on your own terms and remind others that mystery in itself holds a form of power. When you share something people listen because they know your words are chosen carefully.

Hood

Reference: Station 4 - Persona

6 - Shawl

The Shawl is the Persona of care and comfort. You are gentle and emotionally welcoming. People can sense this when you are near. Through your expressed energy, people are graced with a sense of safety in your company and they will turn to you in times of need.

The Shawl Persona forms through empathy and responsibility. You have learned to soothe and support others by sense without having to be asked. Instead of armor, The Shawl shares kindness to shelter. You offer harmony, relief and often put others first without hesitation.

In misalignment, The Shawl Persona can lead to emotional depletion as you overextend and suppress your own needs. It can be easy to lose yourself when you are always showing up for someone else.

When aligned, The Shawl becomes the essence of sacred care. As you lead with compassion you will also receive it as you move through the world with generosity and kindness.

Shawl

Reference: Station 4 - Persona

7 - The Cowl

The Cowl is the Persona of introspection. To others you appear quiet and inwardly focused. You speak little but your words carry weight. There's a stillness about you that feels otherworldly.

The Cowl Persona forms in those who value internal reflection over reaction. The Cowl shields your internal landscape, allowing you to observe and process at your own pace. Often you will communicate through subtle cues and gestures rather than overt expressions.

In misalignment, The Cowl Persona can slip into isolation. You might withdraw to avoid vulnerability or hold back to prevent being misunderstood. Others may perceive this silence as detachment, when in truth it's used as protection.

When aligned, The Cowl engages when it matters, revealing your inner self with selectivity and care. Your mystique models the wisdom of restraint and shows that internal reflection is a powerful form of connection.

Cowl

Reference: Station 4 - Persona

8 - The Crown

The Crown is the Persona of command. You carry yourself with confidence and are a natural leader. Even when you're not seeking power, others defer to you. You are composed, capable and someone who steps forward when a situation needs direction.

This Persona projects structure and status. It's not about ego, it's about decisions and outcomes. You always show up polished and your energy sets the tone of the room. Others rely on your presence often without even realizing it.

In misalignment, The Crown can become less of a leader and more of a controller. You appear distant and over-manage people and situations to protect your own image. Authority becomes your armor instead of your offering.

In alignment, The Crown becomes your steady guide leading with certainty. You don't need to dominate to prove yourself, your presence and track record speak for you. This Persona earns respect without demanding it.

Crown

Reference: Station 4 - Persona

9 - The Halo

The Halo is The Persona of light. You appear to others as luminous, elevated and untouchable. There's just something about your presence that uplifts without effort, as if your very being carries a frequency that others are aspiring for. Through heartfelt and powerful words, you leave a lasting impression rooted in compassion and moral clarity.

The Halo Persona reflects how you embody grace, values and hope in public. You are admired for your wisdom and gentle conviction. You carry yourself with sincerity and emotional maturity.

In misalignment, The Halo can create distance between you and others. They will start to idolize you to the point of disconnection assuming that you are above struggle. You may start to hide your own needs or pain behind this mask as you hide behind the light others expect you to maintain.

When aligned, The Halo Persona is an effortless beacon. You don't need to try to inspire, your truth speaks for itself. You become a mirror showing people their best selves because your light always shines with authenticity.

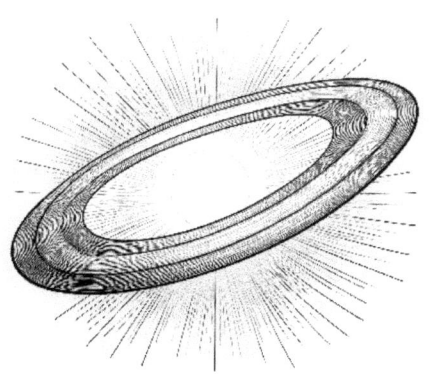

Halo

Reference: Station 4 - Persona

1 - Dependency

Dependency is the internal pull to relinquish your power. It shows up as self-doubt, indecision and by constantly seeking permission from others. You may shape yourself to conform to other people's needs. You may also feel lost without guidance or believe that you cannot function alone. This Inhibition often grows from unresolved relational wounds or abandonment.

When this Inhibition dominates, you become overly attached and easily manipulated. You may delay your own growth by waiting for someone to rescue you. Left unchecked Dependency can turn into stagnation disguised as safety.

Healing this Inhibition begins with self-trust. You must try to relearn that you are able to live life by your own terms. You don't have to do this alone, but recognize when your support system is scaffolding and when it becomes a cage.

Strengthening Opportunities:
- Letting go of people pleasing patterns
- Reclaiming autonomy
- Fortifying your personal decision making power

Dependency

Reference: Station 5 - Inhibition

2 - Selfishness

This Inhibition is not just about greed, it is the fear of scarcity. Selfishness presents itself as a deep belief that vulnerability will invite loss. It will ultimately end in depletion leading to a behavior of withholding energy, time and love.

As this Inhibition takes hold interdependence looks like weakness. Collaboration feels like a trap. You may convince yourself that building walls around yourself is bravery when in fact it is self-isolation.

Healing this Inhibition starts with being open, sharing and trusting without losing yourself. Learn to see connection as nourishment instead of a threat. Vulnerability can become a strength when it's a choice and not forced upon you. When you start giving because you feel safe and steady enough to share, you will begin to understand that connection is a form of wealth.

Strengthening Opportunities:
- Replacing walls with healthy boundaries
- Transforming fear of scarcity into trust in abundance
- Practicing generosity without self erasure

Selfishness

Reference: Station 5 - Inhibition

3 - Apathy

The Apathy Inhibition is the soul's shutdown response when emotion begins to feel too risky or pointless. It will dull sensation and erase purpose. Passion will be replaced with detachment. This Inhibition takes hold in times of burnout and in times of emotional stress. It's not that you don't care, the care has just been buried.

Once Apathy has taken root life appears gray and effort seems foolish. You learn to mask your Apathy through sarcasm, indifference and cold intellect, but underneath it all is a wound that needs healing. Apathy protects you from disappointment by limiting your desire.

The way out of Apathy begins with taking a risk to feel again. You don't need to ignite all of your passion at once, just see what a spark will do at first. Reconnection will happen in moments where you choose curiosity over cynicism and sensation over shutdown. As you allow life to flow through you again, meaning will start to return.

Strengthening Opportunities:
- Reawaken emotion through small acts of active presence
- Replace numbness with intentional engagement
- Find meaning in lived experience

Apathy

$\bigvee$

Reference: Station 5 - Inhibition

4 - Chaos

The Chaos Inhibition is rebellion against order, even in times where order might actually help. It's your inner storm that resists planning, discipline and predictability. While spontaneity can sometimes be a gift, in this extreme it becomes a source of volatility.

When Chaos takes hold stability will feel like you are being controlled and held down. Boundaries will make you feel trapped. You will begin to sabotage your routines and reject authority before it can reject you. Freedom becomes the ultimate goal, but directionless freedom leads to fragmentation.

Recovering from Chaos does not have to mean absolute order. It comes from learning how to channel your wild side into something concrete that lasts. Structure will begin to look like a container for your fire, and not a confinement. In this setting your spontaneity will become a creative force, not a form of self destruction.

Strengthening Opportunities:
- Make it a point during the day to complete small repeatable actions
- Redefine freedom as a choice, not avoidance
- Build trust in structure through consistent follow through

Chaos

Reference: Station 5 - Inhibition

5 - Obligation

Obligation is the weight you feel from unspoken contracts and the inherited roles and responsibilities that leave little room for joy. You learn that worth is earned through sacrifice and that resting is selfish. This Inhibition teaches you that saying yes is safer than being honest.

As the Obligation Inhibition takes control service will turn into servitude. You will begin to believe that your value is tied to how much you do for others, and you will give too much in the effort to keep the peace. The more you give, the more invisible you will feel.

Recovering from this Inhibition begins when you acknowledge that saying no doesn't mean you are being selfish. You are allowed to prioritize what fuels your desires, not just what is expected of you. When you stop giving too much in an attempt to prove your worth, you will allow space for your authentic self.

Strengthening Opportunities:
- Practice saying no without needing to justify it
- Replace the phrase "I have to" with "I choose to"
- Reconnect with things that bring you joy

Obligation

Reference: Station 5 - Inhibition

6 - Neglect

The Neglect Inhibition is about the absence of care. This Neglect can be towards yourself, relationships or even responsibilities. This Inhibition convinces you that detachment is easier than engagement and that not showing up is easier than participation. You will grow numb and withdraw from things that need attending.

As Neglect grows roots, connections will feel more like a burden than a blessing. You will not only ignore your own needs, but also the needs of others. The world becomes a place you are simply passing through, rather than a place you participate in. Distance will become your form of protection.

Healing from this Inhibition begins with understanding that care doesn't cost as much as you thought. Small intentional acts of care will start to break this Inhibition down. You will learn that attention given and attention received from others is a gift. Showing up for your own life will no longer feel like a drain, it will bring joy.

Strengthening Opportunities:
- Start to show small acts of care with consistency
- Replace patterns of avoidance with acts of presence
- Reconnect with the world by awakening your senses

Neglect

Reference: Station 5 - Inhibition

7 - Shallowness

The Shallow Inhibition is about the fear of discovering what lies in the depths. It clings to appearances, rehearsed roles and the safety in being superficial. It keeps you looking polished, but hollow inside, never revealing your true self.

In the grip of Shallowness, life becomes a performance, vulnerability feels like a threat and introspection feels like quicksand. You will hide behind charisma, status and perfectionism to avoid confronting the real world. Everything is curated by you and your heart feels empty.

Healing from Shallowness begins with being honest with yourself. You don't have to transform your false image all at once, but start asking yourself what truth lies beneath it. When you stop performing and start being your true self you will feel a shift, you will discover that unfiltered is the most magnetic version of yourself.

Strengthening Opportunities:
- Trade perfectionism for sincerity one small thing at a time
- Reflect daily about what felt real vs what felt performative
- Engage in activities where no one is watching

Shallowness

Reference: Station 5 - Inhibition

8 - Stagnation

The Stagnation Inhibition is the slow suffocation of potential. Stagnation disguises itself as comfort and logic, but underneath it's actually fear. Fear of both failure and success, and you will feel trapped in ice. Stagnation is something you can escape, but you are stuck because you don't think you can.

When Stagnation has a hold on you every path will appear blocked and inspiration will begin to fade. Procrastinating becomes the norm and you will start to overthink and underact. You will rely on old excuses that once felt true, but now feel hollow. As life drifts by you feel no pull or push from it.

Leaving Stagnation behind comes from movement. You don't even need to know the final destination, just break up the stillness. Momentum will build when you start to act before you are fully ready and by trusting that clarity will follow engagement. When you are able to reclaim the role as a participant in your own life, possibility will again begin to stir.

Strengthening Opportunities:
- Set yourself small time bound goals
- Interrupt familiar routines with intentional change
- Focus on completion not perfection

Stagnation

N

Reference: Station 5 - Inhibition

9 - Isolation

The Isolation Inhibition is the silent wall that not only blocks the world out, but keeps you locked in as well. Sometimes Isolation is actively chosen while other times it may be unconsciously chosen, either way it's a belief that no one can truly understand you and that you are safer alone. Isolation offers the illusion of protection but breeds loneliness and emotional distance.

When Isolation takes root, connection will start to feel dangerous and vulnerability will be mistaken for weakness. You will retreat inward convincing yourself that no one gets it, or if they tried they would just end up leaving in the end. The fear of being misunderstood will become more powerful than the desire to be known.

Healing from Isolation begins with risking connection. You don't have to jump in and bare all, but take steps to let someone in. Bit by bit trust will be rebuilt through shared presence. As you begin to participate you will realize that being seen actually does not weaken you, it reminds you that you are here and you are not meant to carry every burden alone.

Strengthening Opportunities:
- Practice sharing one small thought or feeling a day with someone you can trust
- Say yes to social invitations, even when you would rather hide
- Remind yourself that connection is a skill, not just a feeling

Isolation

Reference: Station 5 - Inhibition

1 - Courage

Courage is the will to move forward even when fear is present. When embodied, Courage shatters the illusion that you must be certain before you can begin. It teaches you to trust action over delay and presence over preparation. This virtue shows up when the path is unclear but the steps still need to be taken.

Courage is your fire in the dark, the energy that propels you to grow. When you walk with courage, you start walking your own path even when it's unproven or misunderstood.

When facing an inhibition Courage reminds you that taking action can create clarity and lead to liberation. You'll know your Courage is rising when you choose to speak the truth, even when your voice shakes, when you choose action without needing permission, and when you stop apologizing for needing more.

Courage

Reference: Station 6 - Core Virtue

2 - Compassion

Compassion is the soft strength that not only heals the self, but can also heal others. True compassion can sit with pain without absorbing it.

The Compassion Virtue bridges the gap between truth and tenderness. It silences your internal critic and brings mercy to the jagged edges of life. Compassion reminds you that to be human is to always be a work in progress, and that your wholeness does not require perfection.

This Virtue liberates by breaking the cycle of blame. It weakens the reflex to punish, to withdraw and to harden. Compassion reminds you that empathy is strength. With this strength you walk through the world heart first, and your love radiates from you like an unseen aura. Those near you can feel it like a calming breeze that needs no explanation.

When facing Inhibition, Compassion leads you towards care without a need for co-dependence. Compassion tells you that it's possible to love while still keeping boundaries, and that it's okay to grieve and grow at the same time. Compassion reveals itself when you are able to give yourself grace without judgment, when you listen without feeling the need to defend, and when you care for others without abandoning yourself.

Compassion

Reference: Station 6 - Core Virtue

3 - Resilience

The Resilience Virtue is the steady force that carries you through uncertainty. Despite any hardships, Resilience keeps moving forward and answers only to the part of you that refuses to disappear.

Resilience is not resistance. It transforms hardship and pain into progress. Resilience allows you to know that failing does not mean failure unless you refuse to rise.

Resilience guards you against defeatism and despair. It changes the internal narrative from "this broke me" to "this helped shape me". The Resilience Virtue liberates by removing shame from struggle and allowing growth to bloom.

To face Inhibition, Resilience teaches you that you don't always have to be ready, you just need to be able to begin again. It enables you to know that although life may weather you, it will never take your will unless you give it away. Resilience is surfacing when you show up even when things are not ideal, when you allow your wounds to become your wisdom, and when you trust that every moment is meaningful no matter how small.

Resilience

Reference: Station 6 - Core Virtue

4 - Integrity

Integrity is the alignment between what you believe and how you live. It's about consistency of character like telling the truth even when a lie would be easier.

The Integrity Virtue is your guide in an uncertain world full of manipulation, masks and shortcuts. It asks not for perfection, but for truth that comes from within and always walks beside you.

This Virtue liberates by cutting through the fog and removing the weight of pretending. When you live with Integrity there is no story to keep straight and no mask to maintain.

When Integrity is facing Inhibition, it becomes your restoration. It reminds you that peace doesn't come from people pleasing, it comes from honoring your own core truth regardless of outcome. Integrity is making itself known when you speak the truth even when it's uncomfortable, when you choose actions that match your own values, and when you no longer sacrifice your authenticity for acceptance.

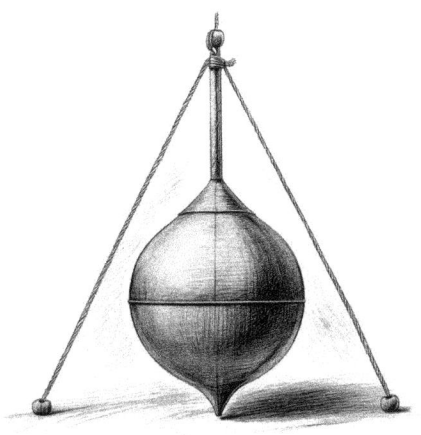

Integrity

Reference: Station 6 - Core Virtue

5 - Wisdom

The Wisdom Virtue is not inherited, it's something that you earn through life experience. While knowledge can be memorized, Wisdom on the other hand is metabolized. Wisdom peers deep within seeing far beyond the surface and it slows you down in a world that's always rushing. It helps us maintain the bigger picture mentality and act with patience. The qualities of Wisdom not only benefit you, they also benefit those close to you.

The Wisdom Virtue can see through the smoke and liberates by revealing the meaning behind it. It takes your struggle and uses the experience to add to its bottomless pool. Your pain becomes insight, your detour becomes redirection.

When facing Inhibition Wisdom shows you how to pause for a moment, reflect and respond instead of just reacting. It teaches us that growth is not about speed, it's about depth. Your Wisdom is active when you trust your timing and accept outcomes, when you not only seek a solution but also seek to understand, and when you see value in challenges you have endured.

Wisdom

Reference: Station 6 - Core Virtue

6 - Devotion

Devotion is not about obligation, it's about commitment. It's the choice to pour your time, love and energy into something beyond momentary desire. When life becomes uneasy, the Devotion Virtue draws from the deepest region of the self and gives you clear focus.

This Virtue is a form of inner clarity. A knowing of what deserves your time and energy, and giving it your full allegiance. This virtue can transform distraction into discipline, uncertainty into presence and wavering into strength.

When facing Inhibition Devotion can take a cluster of scattered energy and condense it into focus. Devotion doesn't ask you to serve everything, but the things you do choose are served truly and deeply. Devotion is active when you act from purpose before pleasure, when you stay when your instinct is to run, and when you build rituals around what you love.

Devotion

Reference: Station 6 - Core Virtue

85

7 - Authenticity

Authenticity is the virtue of presenting yourself just as you are, no distortions, no performances and no disguises. Authenticity is not just honesty, it's also integrity of self. When this Virtue is alive inside you it brings your actions, voice and values all into harmony with each other. In this form you no longer bend to belong, you become the shape that defines the room.

To walk with the Authenticity Virtue can sometimes feel vulnerable, but it invites you to bring your true self fully. It doesn't demand perfection, only honesty.

When facing Inhibition Authenticity uses the truth to set you free, even when it's messy. It's the courage that stays consistent with your soul. Your Authenticity is rising when you stop apologizing for who you are, when you feel comfortable and grounded with your presence, and when you speak and act in accordance with your truth.

Authenticity

Reference: Station 6 - Core Virtue

8 - Adaptability

The Adaptability Virtue is not about being passive and accepting change, it's about dancing with it. It never asks you to abandon yourself when life shifts, it reminds you to stay rooted in who you are while adjusting your rhythm and pivot without panic. Adaptability is grace under pressure, flexibility without collapse.

Adaptability forges new pathways, it doesn't cling to how things should be, it responds to how things are. With clarity and creative force Adaptability reminds us to remember the difference between being rigid and being flexible.

Adaptability is about molding yourself while also staying true to yourself in times of evolving circumstances. In this way even when things change you are there and ready with your best foot forward.

When facing Inhibition Adaptability becomes the key to remind you that change is not the enemy, it can be a medium where transformation occurs. Adaptability is active when you respond instead of react, when you can shift roles or plans without losing your center, and when you can view change as a creative force instead of a threat.

Adaptability

Reference: Station 6 - Core Virtue

9 - Vision

Vision is the Virtue of foresight. It's an internal drive that pulls you beyond your current limitations. Vision is about holding your current state steady while also seeing clearly what it could be. Vision doesn't just provide clarity, it also restores meaning. In moments of struggle or confusion Vision reminds you why you began and reconnects you to your long-term purpose. It keeps your journey moving towards the destination even if the middle feels messy.

To embody Vision is to trust the unfolding, when hardship presents itself you don't only see it, you can also see through it. You know that when a challenge arises in no way is that the end of your journey.

When facing Inhibition, Vision provides clarity when something is clouding your path. Vision becomes the beacon in the distance keeping you pointed towards your goals. Your vision is active when you can see meaning in setbacks, when you hold space for the future without rushing it, and when you act in service of something larger than yourself.

Vision

Reference: Station 6 - Core Virtue

1 - Renewal

"I am the one who begins again"
Self-Starting, Empowered, Reclaimed

This Inspiration reminds you of your ability to reset, not just habits and circumstances, but the entire relationship with the self. It reminds you that you are not bound by old choices, you are the one who has the power to turn the page. You have the power to begin a new chapter when the moment demands it.

New beginnings are not handed out by the world, they are claimed by you. Whatever the circumstance you find yourself in, if the time comes to begin again that decision is yours to make.

Call upon this Inspiration when you feel stuck, unworthy or behind. Let it remind you that you can never be too far gone to begin again, and that you do not need permission to do so.

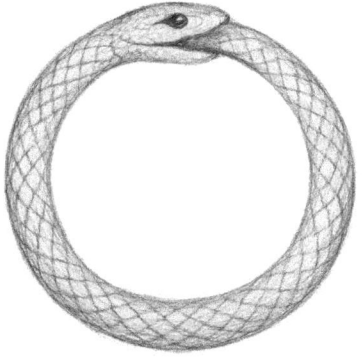

Renewal

Reference: Station 7 - Inspiration

2 - Unity

"I am part of the greater whole"
Empathetic, Perceptive, Receptive

This Inspiration comes to you when you feel disconnected from others, purpose or even yourself. Unity reminds you that sensitivity is not a weakness, it's how you hear what is unspoken. It's how you feel the things that others hold inside.

To embody Unity is to return to the great web, the living pattern that connects all things. You are not here to carry the world, only to find the place you belong within it. You are a thread in the unseen design, a signal moving through the resonance of the whole.

Call upon this Inspiration when the noise of separation grows too loud. Let it remind you that harmony is not something you chase, it's something you return to.

Unity

Reference: Station 7 - Inspiration

3 - Joy

"My joy is sacred"
Creative, Visionary, Expressive

This Inspiration reclaims your inner creativity. The part of you that shines not because you need to impress, but because it's how you breathe. Joy is not a luxury or a performance. It's a current that moves through you when you allow yourself to feel deeply, speak truth and create at will.

Your joy is a force that opens hearts and minds. When you let this Inspiration rise you become a source of brightness in a dim world by showing others what it's like to be alive and awake. Your spark gives others a nudge to find their own Joy.

Call upon this Inspiration when you feel distant or drained. Let it remind you that pleasure is part of your power. When you return to what lights you up, the world brightens too.

Joy

Reference: Station 7 - Inspiration

4 - Sincerity

"What I build reflects who I am"
Authentic, Grounded, Aligned

This Inspiration calls you into harmony between what you believe and how you live. Sincerity is not about perfection, it's about staying true to yourself. When you embody it, your actions and heart are in line even when no one else is watching. Honesty becomes a source of strength rather than a form of control.

Sincerity is your anchor. It gives you a center that never wavers when the world pulls at you. You become trustworthy to yourself and others. The relationships and values you build begin to reflect something real and enduring.

Call upon this Inspiration when you feel scattered, uncertain or tempted to bend your values to fit in. Let it remind you to return to what's steady. When you hold your ground with consistency, you show others what strength really looks like.

Sincerity

Reference: Station 7 - Inspiration

5 - Change

"Change is my ally, not my enemy"
Unbound, Brave, Moving

This Inspiration is about your capacity to evolve by choice. You sense when something no longer fits and when you have the courage to step beyond the known. Change doesn't need to wait until you are forced into it, this is the power of initiating your own growth.

To embody Change is to embrace the unknown. You allow yourself to outgrow something that once defined you. At this juncture you are choosing expanse over repetition.

Call upon this Inspiration when you feel stuck in old roles or when you feel unsure of what's next. Let it remind you that your direction is your own to claim, and every step forward shapes the path beneath your feet.

Change

Reference: Station 7 - Inspiration

6 - Love

"Love is the root of my strength"
Devoted, Rooted, Caring

This Inspiration draws you in to what you cherish most. Love is the choice to stay connected, to offer yourself with intention, and to build from a place of meaning.

To embody love is to show up with genuine care. It presents itself in the way you commit, in your actions and in the energy you offer without needing recognition. Love becomes real when you make the choice to invest in it fully, even when it's difficult.

Call upon this Inspiration when you feel unappreciated, disconnected or worn thin. Let it remind you that your care carries weight and that offering love with your whole heart is a strength not a sacrifice.

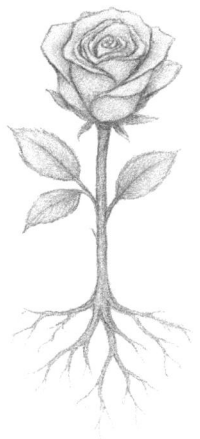

Love

Reference: Station 7 - Inspiration

7 - Reflection

"Stillness holds answers"
Observant, Quiet, Interwoven

This Inspiration invites you inward into the space where silence speaks. It asks you to perceive through symbols, feelings and subtle impressions. Reflection doesn't rush to interpret, it allows meaning to reveal itself slowly.

To embody Reflection is to become familiar with the quiet. It's found in the way you notice the things that others miss, and the way you carry the questions with you that don't need immediate answers. Dreams and metaphors become your language as you remain patient and wait for clarity to reveal itself.

Call upon this Inspiration when the world seems confusing. Let it remind you that answers often arrive when you stop chasing them. In stillness the things that matter most will rise to meet you.

Reflection

Reference: Station 7 - Inspiration

8 - Resilience

"I adapt, but I do not vanish"
Composed, Certain, Self-Commanding

This Inspiration reveals the strength that comes from inner steadiness. Resilience is about staying present throughout change. You build authority by showing up, without needing to defend or explain your place.

To embody Resilience is to move with intention. You adjust when needed but never disappear. There's a calm force in how you hold your values, speak your truth and remain composed even when things can feel uncertain.

Call upon this Inspiration when you feel overlooked or ungrounded. Let it remind you that staying true to yourself is its own form of power. You are not here to disappear, you are here to remain.

Resilience

Reference: Station 7 - Inspiration

9 - Radiance

"I see beyond the present moment"
Wise, Quiet, Expansive

This Inspiration is your reminder that presence itself can be powerful. Your wisdom comes from lived experience and the way you listen, notice and understand brings light into the world.

To embody Radiance is to see clearly across time. You keep perspective even when others lose their way. The depth of your insight steadies those around you, and your calm presence invites others to slow down and remember what matters.

Call upon this Inspiration when the world feels rushed. Let it remind you that your wisdom doesn't need to announce itself, it shines in the way you see, feel and hold space.

Radiance

Reference: Station 7 - Inspiration

1 - The Evolved Seeker

The Evolved Seeker is no longer restless, they are radiant in their direction. They see things with clarity and no longer feel haunted about what they might be missing. Every journey now is a return to truth, not an escape from discomfort. Their path is self made and their presence is magnetic. Stillness is no longer feared, it has become a source of power, not stagnation.

Through facing and overcoming Inhibition, The Evolved Seeker learns that running is not the same thing as freedom. They learn to chase direction without panic, to act without fleeing and to stay connected even while moving ahead.

The Evolved Seeker inspires others by simply being. They are able to map uncharted futures and show how self-trust leads to self-realization. The Evolved Seeker's life leaves a trail for others to follow

Signs of Evolution:
- Knows when to move and when to rest
- Listens inward before acting outward
- Anchored in freedom that doesn't require escape
- Offers direction without demand

Seeker

Reference: Station 8 - Evolved Archetypes

2 - The Evolved Emissary

The Evolved Emissary no longer needs to walk a tightrope to keep the peace. Their presence can bridge opposites not by avoiding conflict, but by honoring differences. Their silence is potent and when they speak their words are deliberate. This version of the self is no longer trapped in the role of an intermediary. Instead they have become a channel for reconciliation, wisdom and clarity.

Having faced Inhibition, The Evolved Emissary has learned that true connection requires boundaries just as much as openness. This Evolved version of self no longer dissolves their own identity when aiming to please others, instead they learn to mirror - reflecting back possibility, perspective and shared humanity.

Signs of Evolution:
- Speaks truth without tipping scales
- Connects without self-erasing
- Creates safe space for tension to unravel
- Holds paradox with ease and empathy

Emissary

Reference: Station 8 - Evolved Archetypes

3 - The Evolved Muse

The Evolved Muse doesn't stop at stirring emotions, they give them shape. They have moved beyond the volatility of raw expression and into a steadier radiance. Their creativity has matured. They know how to receive inspiration without burning out, and how to inspire others without losing themselves.

After facing Inhibition, The Evolved Muse has learned that emotion is not the enemy, it's the instrument. The Muse now refines their gifts into a true form. Their joy becomes service and their voice becomes medicine.

The Evolved Muse doesn't perform to gain approval, they create because they must and because the things they express help others remember beauty, possibility and soul. Through art, storytelling, movement and presence The Evolved Muse leaves color in their wake.

Signs of Evolution:
- Channels inspiration without depletion
- Creates with intention, not for reaction
- Uses joy as a tool for healing
- Honors both expression and rest

Muse

Reference: Station 8 - Evolved Archetypes

4 - The Evolved Warden

The Evolved Warden is no longer bound by rigidity. They have transmuted control into stewardship, turning their love of order into a gift rather than a cage. This version of The Warden doesn't just build walls, they create sanctuaries. They understand when to protect, when to let go, and when to lead without domination.

After confronting Inhibition, The Evolved Warden learned how to flow within form. Discipline becomes devotion, structure becomes soul-aligned. They no longer fear disruption, because they trust what they have built can bend without breaking.

The Evolved Warden cultivates resilience in the world around them. People look up to them not for rules, but for rhythm. With grounded vision, the steadiness of The Warden can calm a storm.

Signs of Evolution:
- Uses structure as a tool for liberation
- Balances tradition with intuitive timing
- Leads through quiet example, not force
- Creates safe spaces for others to grow

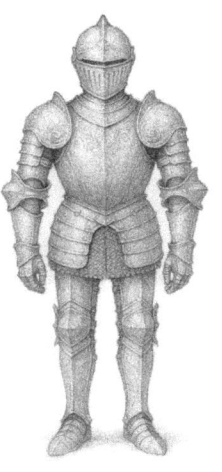

Warden

Reference: Station 8 - Evolved Archetypes

5 - The Evolved Wanderer

The Evolved Wanderer is no longer lost to the wind, they have become the wind. The Wanderer has learned the difference between escape and exploration. They now move not to avoid, but to experience. Their life has become a dance with possibility.

Rooted in freedom and matured by reflection, The Evolved Wanderer trusts the unfolding of their path. No longer do they run from discomfort or commitment, they have learned to stay long enough to feel the truth before moving on with intention. Their adaptability has become a compass, not a crutch.

The Evolved Wanderer inspires others to break from limitation with grace. They hold space for change while also honoring the lessons learned in the past. They are trailblazers of a different kind now, not just seekers of novelty, but stewards of meaningful transformation.

Signs of Evolution:
- Moves through life with presence and purpose
- Honors both roots and wings
- Teaches that freedom isn't fleeing, it's alignment
- Lives fully in each moment, knowing it too will pass

Wanderer

Reference: Station 8 - Evolved Archetypes

6 - The Evolved Guardian

The Evolved Guardian embodies a love that is no longer self-erasing. In their previous form The Guardian sacrificed too much, but in evolved form they now know that true protection begins with self-preservation. Their devotion becomes a conscious choice, not a compulsion. They love boldly, not blindly.

Through their experience The Evolved Guardian has learned that care doesn't mean carrying everything. They now protect without controlling, support without enabling, and serve without forgetting their own needs. They embody a sacred steadiness, one that holds space without absorbing pain.

The Evolved Guardian becomes a guiding light others look to for grounding. Their quiet strength creates a safe space for transformation to happen. They teach through example, showing that the strongest form of love is the one rooted in self respect.

Signs of Evolution:
- Knows when to step in, and when to stand back
- Protects the sacred space of others and their own
- Offers a love that empowers
- Moves from duty to devotion

Guardian

Reference: Station 8 - Evolved Archetypes

7 - The Evolved Weaver

The Evolved Weaver no longer hides in the realm of the unseen. Instead of sitting in a state of an observer, they now begin to participate. Their insight learned has turned into action. They weave from within, no longer stuck in a state of endless introspection. Their reflection now becomes revelation.

The Evolved Weaver trusts their timing and speaks with clarity. Their inner life becomes a tool, not a trap. They now have space for inner paradox without needing resolution or certainty.

The Evolved Weaver becomes a quiet oracle, people are drawn to them for their deep wisdom. Their ability to articulate the intangible leaves a mark that people remember. They don't just see the deeper currents, they show others how to listen. Their life has become a bridge between silence and expression.

Signs of Evolution:
- Shares insight with courage and clarity
- No longer fears being seen
- Translates the invisible into form
- Lives in harmony with mystery, not in fear of it

Weaver

Reference: Station 8 - Evolved Archetypes

8 - The Evolved Magnate

The Evolved Magnate has moved beyond accumulation and control. They are no longer driven by ego and dominance. Their strategic gifts are now used for something larger than themselves, impact replaces image, legacy replaces the pursuit of legacy-building and their empire becomes a living offering.

This Evolved version of the self has shed the need to possess, compete or control. Now having learned to mentor, structure and support with clarity and strength, their success uplifts and doesn't overshadow. Their influence ripples far beyond personal gain.

The new Magnate leaves behind a lot more than wealth and reputation, they leave behind sustainability, and people they have influenced are far more independent for having known them. The Evolved Magnate doesn't seek credit, they seek positive change. The work is no longer about just climbing, it's about holding a space at the top for others to rise.

Signs of Evolution:
- Uses ambition in service of a collective
- Creates structures that liberate, not limit
- Defines success by impact, not image
- Cultivates other leaders rather than commanding followers

Magnate

Reference: Station 8 - Evolved Archetypes

9 - The Evolved Luminary

The Evolved Luminary has transcended the need to guide, teach or even be seen. Their very presence becomes the transmission. They are no longer concerned with recognition or outcomes. They radiate a quiet power that needs no stage. They are living in the truth that they once sought to speak.

After facing their Inhibition, The Evolved Luminary sheds the identity of the healer and seer. What remains now is an essence of pure awareness and unwavering compassion. They embody trust in the unfolding of all things. Their illumination is not external, it's the light within.

The Evolved Luminary teaches through silence, through being, and through the soft glow left in their wake. They show others how to become themselves by the way they live. Their gift is presence, their offering is peace.

Signs of Evolution:
- Radiate clearly without needing attention
- Uplifts others simply by being themselves
- Holds deep truths with gentleness, not urgency
- Trusts in cycles, timing, and the unseen forces at work

Luminary

Reference: Station 8 - Evolved Archetypes

Archetype Correspondences

1 - Seeker

Planet: Mars - Embodies action, willpower, and the drive to forge new paths
Element: Fire - Bold, initiating, passionate, and restless in pursuit of growth
Color: Crimson - Represents courage, movement, and primal instinct
Animal: Wolf - A lone navigator guided by instinct, loyalty to path over pack, and a hunger for discovery
Wood: Birch - Symbol of new beginnings, exploration, and the courage to change paths
Herb: Ginger - Stimulates movement, ignites action, and dispels fear with fiery momentum
Gemstone: Red Jasper - Grounds restless energy while fueling courage and endurance for the journey ahead

2 - Emissary

Planet: Venus - Brings harmony, beauty, and the art of connection
Element: Air - Flexible, thoughtful, and guided by reason and exchange
Color: Rose Gold - Symbolizes grace, empathy, and equilibrium
Animal: Dove - A calm presence that bridges opposing forces with gentleness and unwavering inner peace
Wood: Dogwood - gentleness, diplomacy, and subtle strength
Herb: Lemon Balm - Calms tension, enhances clarity, and supports compassionate communication
Gemstone: Blue Lace Agate - Encourages gentle expression, harmonizes relationships, and soothes inner conflict

3 - Muse

Planet: Mercury - Symbolizes communication, performance, and creative flow
Element: Water - Emotional, fluid, and constantly transforming
Color: Iridescent Lilac - Represents inspiration, emotion, and the ever-shifting spectrum of beauty
Animal: Hummingbird - A vibrant presence that brings joy, dances through life, and pollinates wonder wherever it lands
Wood: Cherry - Symbol of beauty, playfulness, and creative renewal
Herb: Damiana - Sparks inspiration, lifts the spirit, and supports sensual, expressive energy
Gemstone: Carnelian - Fuels passion, boosts confidence, and empowers artistic expression

4 - Warden

Planet: Saturn - Brings structure, discipline, and long-term vision
Elemental Essence: Earth - Stable, grounded, and tied to physical reality and time-tested truth
Color: Deep Forest Green - Symbolizes endurance, protection, and ancestral strength
Animal: Ox - A patient and tireless guardian, grounded in routine, strength, and steady service
Wood: Oak - Symbol of strength, structure, endurance, and sacred legacy
Herb: Rosemary - Enhances clarity, focus, and memory; protects and preserves order
Gemstone: Hematite - Grounds energy, reinforces discipline, and strengthens inner resolve

5 - Wanderer

Planet: Mercury - Quick, curious, ever-shifting; ruler of travel, thought, and transitions
Element: Air - Represents mental flexibility, movement, freedom, and curiosity
Color: Sky Blue - Reflects openness, mental clarity, and boundless potential
Animal: Swallow - A migratory spirit that carries messages across vast distances, never lingering too long, yet always returning wiser
Wood: Sycamore - connected with journeys, transformation, and adaptability
Herb: Yarrow - travel talisman, boundary setting, and courage in new terrain
Gemstone: Turquoise - protects travelers, supports communication, and fosters clarity

6 - Guardian

Planet: Venus - Embodies care, connection, love, and the drive to nurture and protect
Element: Earth - Stable, dependable, and supportive. Tied to caretaking and endurance
Color: Rose Gold - Soft yet strong, symbolizing love in action and enduring beauty
Animal: Deer - Gentle but alert, guided by empathy, grace, and a protective instinct for those they cherish
Wood: Cedar - represents protection, purification, and sacred connection
Herb: Motherwort - nurturing, heart-protective, symbolic of fierce maternal energy
Gemstone: Smoky Quartz - grounding, shielding, and self-nourishing

Archetype Correspondences

7 - Weaver

Planet: Neptune - Represents dreams, intuition, mysticism, and the dissolving of boundaries
Element: Water - Fluid, introspective, and emotionally attuned; carries the tides of inner wisdom
Color: Indigo - Evokes mystery, depth, and the vision beyond the known
Animal: Owl - Nocturnal observer with deep sight, silent wisdom, and an ability to navigate the hidden
Wood: Willow - Represents intuition, flexibility, ancestral memory, and deep emotional currents
Herb: Mugwort - Enhances dreams, psychic insight, and inner vision. Sacred to seers and travelers of the unseen
Gemstone: Labradorite --Shields the aura, reveals hidden truths, and supports journeys through the subconscious

8 - Magnate

Planet: Saturn - Embodies structure, discipline, legacy, and the mastery earned over time
Element: Earth - Solid, enduring, and focused on tangible manifestation
Color: Deep Gold - Symbolizes wealth, leadership, and the gravity of vision realized
Animal: Stag - Regal, grounded, and commanding. Represents dignity, leadership, and ancestral authority
Wood: Mahogany - symbolizes leadership, power, and legacy through refinement
Herb: Bay Laurel - Enhances clarity, ambition and victorious intention. Used in rites of power and achievement
Gemstone: Pyrite - Embodies confidence, strategic thinking, and magnetism. A powerful stone for manifestation and authority

9 - Luminary

Planet: Neptune - Intuition, transcendence, and the dissolving of ego
Element: Water - Fluid, emotional, and connected to collective healing
Color: Violet - Symbol of spiritual insight, mysticism, and transformation
Animal: Owl - Silent observer of the unseen, wisdom keeper, and nocturnal guide
Wood: Elder - sacred to mystics, represents connection to otherworldly wisdom
Herb: Blue Lotus - Enhances intuition, calms the spirit, and opens pathways to higher consciousness
Gemstone: Amethyst - Amplifies inner wisdom, compassion, and intuitive alignment. A stone of higher consciousness and peace

Archetype Correspondences

Interpreting The Final Sum: Your Personal Frequency Number

Once your cosmic signature is complete, you can optionally calculate your final frequency. It is the sum of all 8 Station numbers then reduced. There are no definitions here. Instead of meanings, I offer you to listen, notice and interpret using your intuition. You may already feel your final sums pull, through dream, memories, symbols, lucky charms and Déjà vu.

Let this number become one of your tools. You can use it in ritual, creative design, when you need focus, energetic grounding etc... you decide how it fits best with you. Let your number show up as a sign when you least expect it. Let it whisper to you on the wind. With the 8 Stations now discovered, embodied and recorded, there remains one final number lying in plain sight.

As you have discovered, each Station reveals a number between 1 and 9. On their own each of these numbers reflect the energy of individual roles, lessons and expressions. When added together they create something different - an energetic current that pulses beneath your Cosmic Signature.

The final number is your Frequency Number

To Calculate the Frequency Number add together the number from each of your eight Stations. Then reduce the number to a single digit using the Pythagorean Numerology system we used earlier by breaking down our names and birth dates in preparation for our journey through the 8 Stations.

Example:

$$3 + 1 + 3 + 7 + 4 + 2 + 9 + 4 + 1 = 34$$

$$3 + 4 = 7$$

Your Final Frequency Number is 7

Your Final Frequency Number is not just a sum. It's a resonance, a distilled echo of your pattern, a hidden thread that weaves through the entire architecture of the self. It's not another Archetype, identity or role. It's a tuning fork, an ambient vibration that returns you to center.

Your Final Frequency Number is not assigned, it's revealed.

Your Cosmic Signature: Next Steps

Ways to Work with Your Frequency Number

- As a Ritual Number - you can use it to structure practices. Light X amount of candles, pull X amount of cards or repeat a mantra X amount of times etc.... Let the number create rhythm and structure for you.

- As a Sigil Anchor - incorporate it into geometry, spacing or repetition. Let it define the angles, point counts or designs of future Sigils.

- As a Time Marker - Look for it in time signatures such as 2:22, 3:33, 4:44 etc... use these moments to ground, affirm or reset.

- As a Grounding Point - When scattered say it aloud, draw it on paper, whisper it softly, whatever feels right to you. Let it act as a tether to clarity.

- As an Energy Signature - See it as your signal, the tone your soul broadcasts when you are fully aligned. Not an energy you chase, but one you return to.

- As a Living Mystery - It may take on a different meaning as you grow. Let it evolve with you. Let it reveal itself again and again.

- As a Sign - Look for it in nature, to appear to you wherever it may and reflect on its meaning.

- As a Meditation Focus - Hold the number in your mind or repeat it silently. Use it like a mantra or visual cue to anchor your awareness.

- As a Personal Rune or Glyph - Design a simple symbol that represents your number. It could be a unique shape, dot pattern, or stroke sequence

There are just some ideas to get you started.
Use your intuition to work with your number in any manner that feels right for you.

Your Cosmic Signature: Next Steps

Sigil Ideas for Next Steps

1. Trace and recreate your Cosmic Signature into a clean Sigil.
   - Draw the final Sigil on a clean piece of paper or The Sigil of Self Sheet without the grid
   - Transfer it to wood, stone, metal or fabric
   - Burn or etch it onto an item
   - Digitize it

2. Carry it with you as a charm
   - Write it down, fold it and tuck it into your wallet, purse or pocket
   - Seal it inside an envelope, charm bag or locket
   - Laminate it and use it as a bookmark or daily reminder

3. Create a ritual around it
   - Meditate while visualizing the Sigil and see what manifests
   - Recite a personal affirmation while tracing the design with your finger
   - Draw the Sigil while visualizing your intent

4. Display it with intention
   - Frame and hang your finished Sigil
   - Add it to a vision board or sacred space
   - Use as a centerpiece for spellwork

5. Integrate it into your creative works
   - Use the Sigil shape in art, poetry or jewelry
   - Incorporate the lines into a tattoo or personal mark
   - Weave the shape into future Sigil work

These are some ideas but you are not bound or restricted by them, be creative and use your Sigil and Frequency number in any way that feels right to you.

The Worksheets

The following worksheets are available for free download at curiohut.com. They are not required but are recommended to make the process easier. If you choose not to download and print them for use you can use the examples here to make your own.

- The Cosmic Signature Worksheet is the main worksheet that will be used during The Sigil Self Journey. Here you will write in your X and Y coordinates. Your Station Numbers and Draw your Sigil lines.

- The Numerology Worksheet can be used to perform name and birth date calculations.

- The Cosmic Signature Sheet can be used to trace your finished Cosmic Signature to a cleaner format while keeping the Station Numbers intact, or use the individual Sigils for each entry in place of the numbers as seen in the lower right corner of the page in the reference section.

- The Sigil of Self Sheet can be used to trace your finished Comic Signature Sigil over to a cleaner format.

Birthdate

Month

Day

Year

Life Path Number (Full Birthdate)

Total

Name

First

Middle

Last

Personality Number (Consonants)

Soul Number (Vowels)

Destiny Number (Full Name)

Total

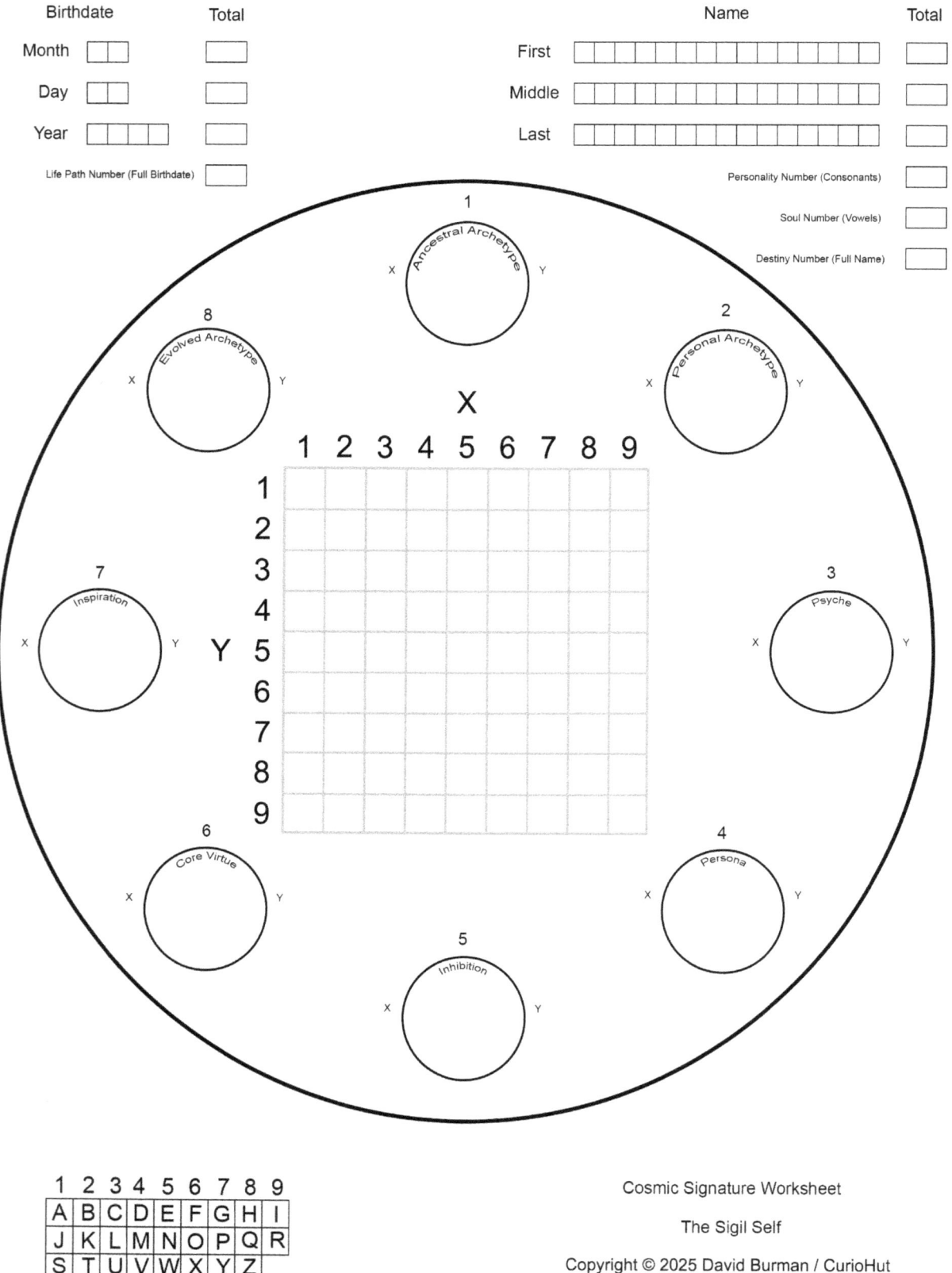

1 Ancestral Archetype
2 Personal Archetype
3 Psyche
4 Persona
5 Inhibition
6 Core Virtue
7 Inspiration
8 Evolved Archetype

X
1 2 3 4 5 6 7 8 9
Y
1 2 3 4 5 6 7 8 9

	1	2	3	4	5	6	7	8	9
A	B	C	D	E	F	G	H	I
J	K	L	M	N	O	P	Q	R
S	T	U	V	W	X	Y	Z	

Cosmic Signature Worksheet

The Sigil Self

Numerology Worksheet

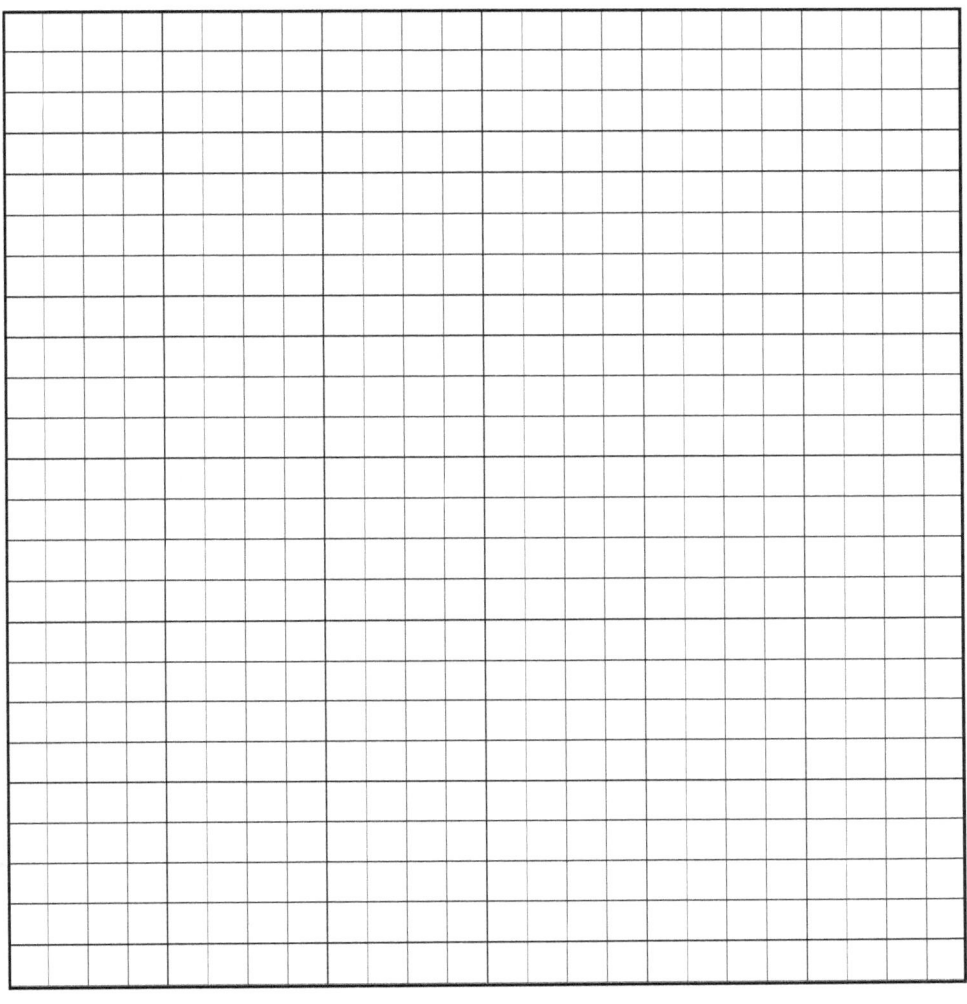

1	2	3	4	5	6	7	8	9
A	B	C	D	E	F	G	H	I
J	K	L	M	N	O	P	Q	R
S	T	U	V	W	X	Y	Z	

Life Path Number = Full Birthdate

Personality Number = Full name consonants

Soul Number = Full Name Vowels

Destiny Number = Full Name Complete

Cosmic Signature

of _____

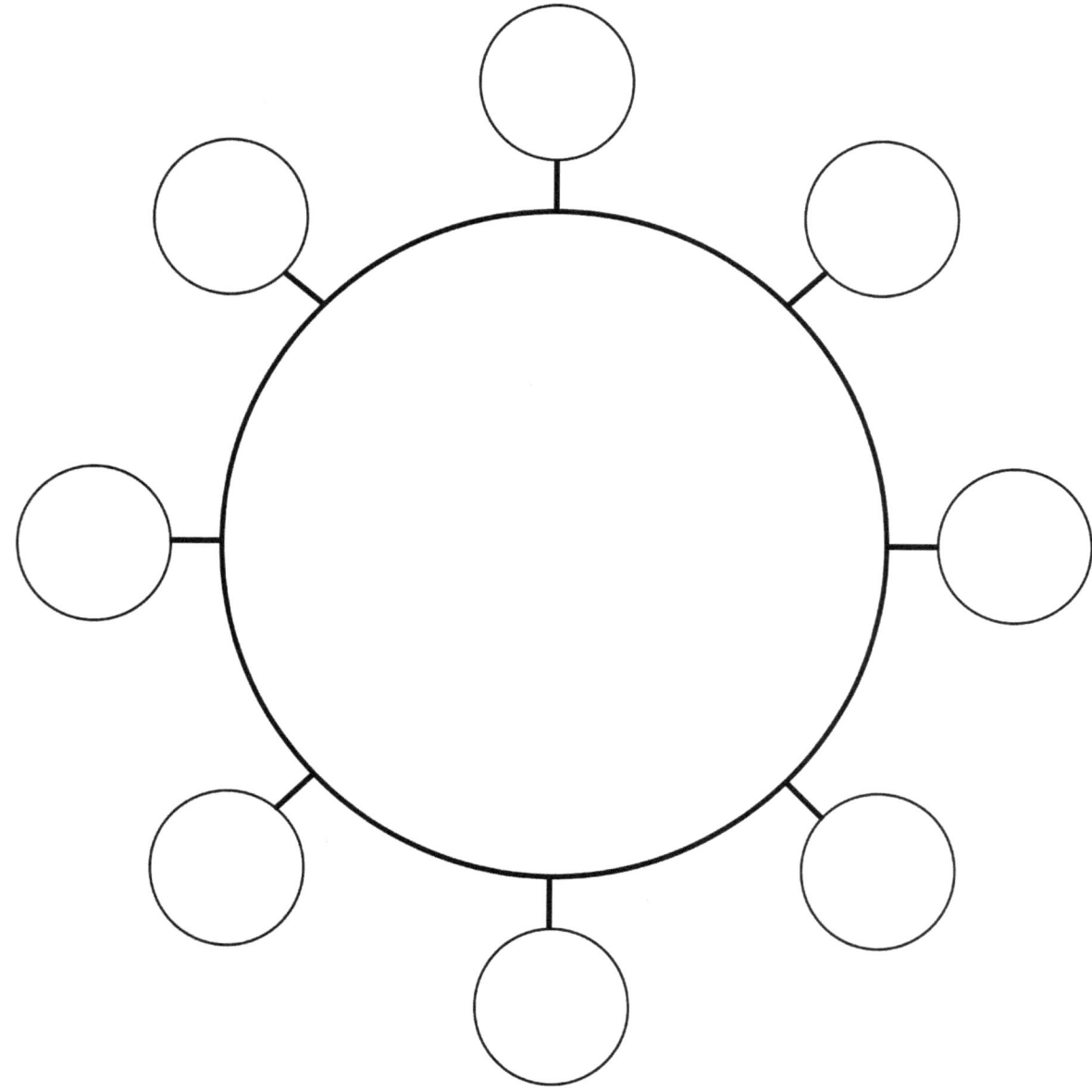

The Sigil of Self

of _____

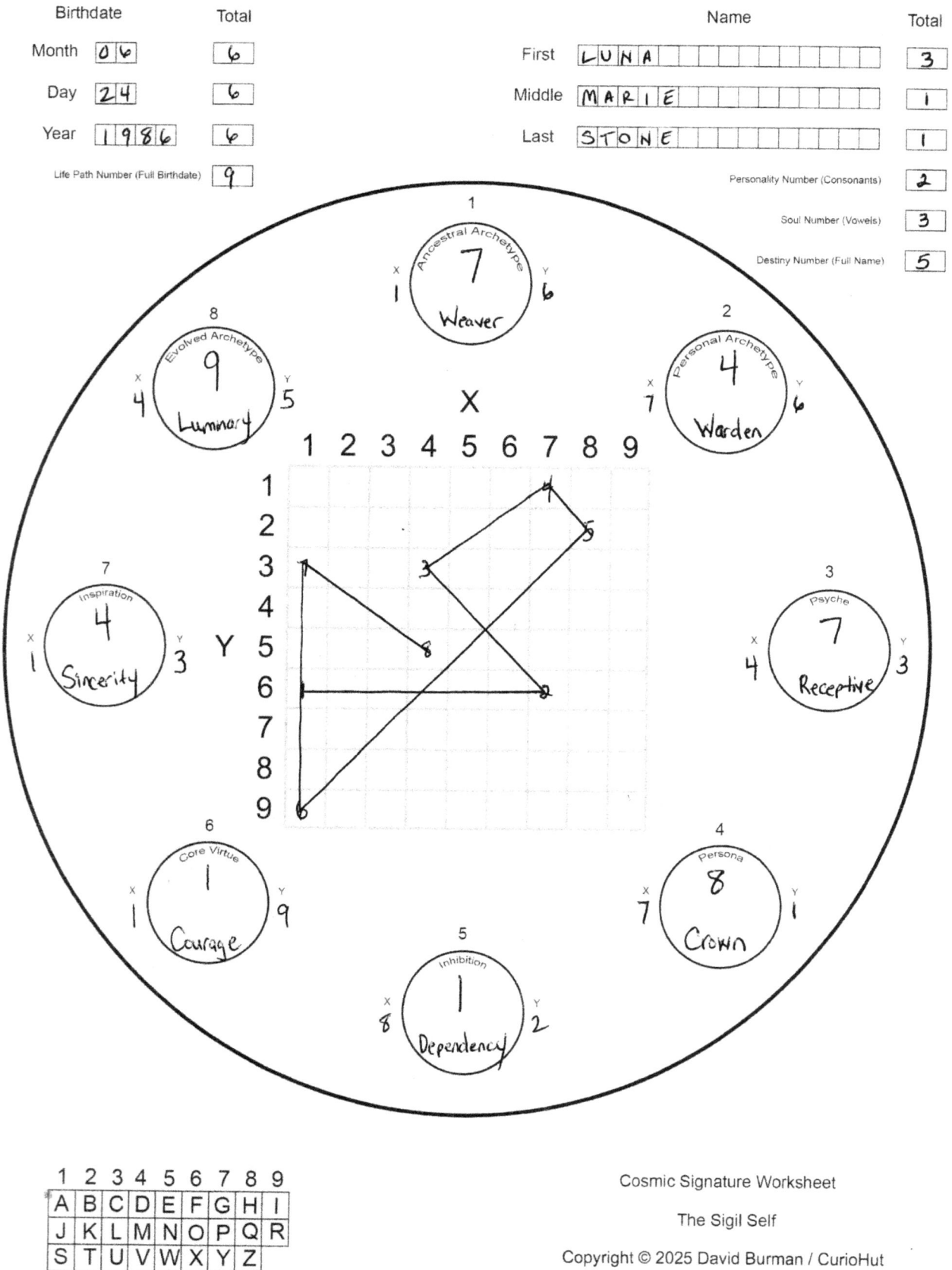

Birthdate

Month `0` `6`   Total `6`

Day `2` `4`   Total `6`

Year `1` `9` `8` `6`   Total `6`

Life Path Number (Full Birthdate) `9`

Name   **Total**

First `L` `U` `N` `A`   `3`

Middle `M` `A` `R` `I` `E`   `1`

Last `S` `T` `O` `N` `E`   `1`

Personality Number (Consonants) `2`

Soul Number (Vowels) `3`

Destiny Number (Full Name) `5`

1 — Ancestral Archetype — 7 — Weaver — X 1 — Y 6

8 — Evolved Archetype — 9 — Luminary — X 4 — Y 5

2 — Personal Archetype — 4 — Warden — X 7 — Y 6

7 — Inspiration — 4 — Sincerity — X 1 — Y 3

3 — Psyche — 7 — Receptive — X 4 — Y 3

6 — Core Virtue — 1 — Courage — X 1 — Y 9

4 — Persona — 8 — Crown — X 7 — Y 1

5 — Inhibition — 1 — Dependency — X 8 — Y 2

X: 1 2 3 4 5 6 7 8 9
Y: 1 2 3 4 5 6 7 8 9

1	2	3	4	5	6	7	8	9
A	B	C	D	E	F	G	H	I
J	K	L	M	N	O	P	Q	R
S	T	U	V	W	X	Y	Z	

Cosmic Signature Worksheet

The Sigil Self

Numerology Worksheet

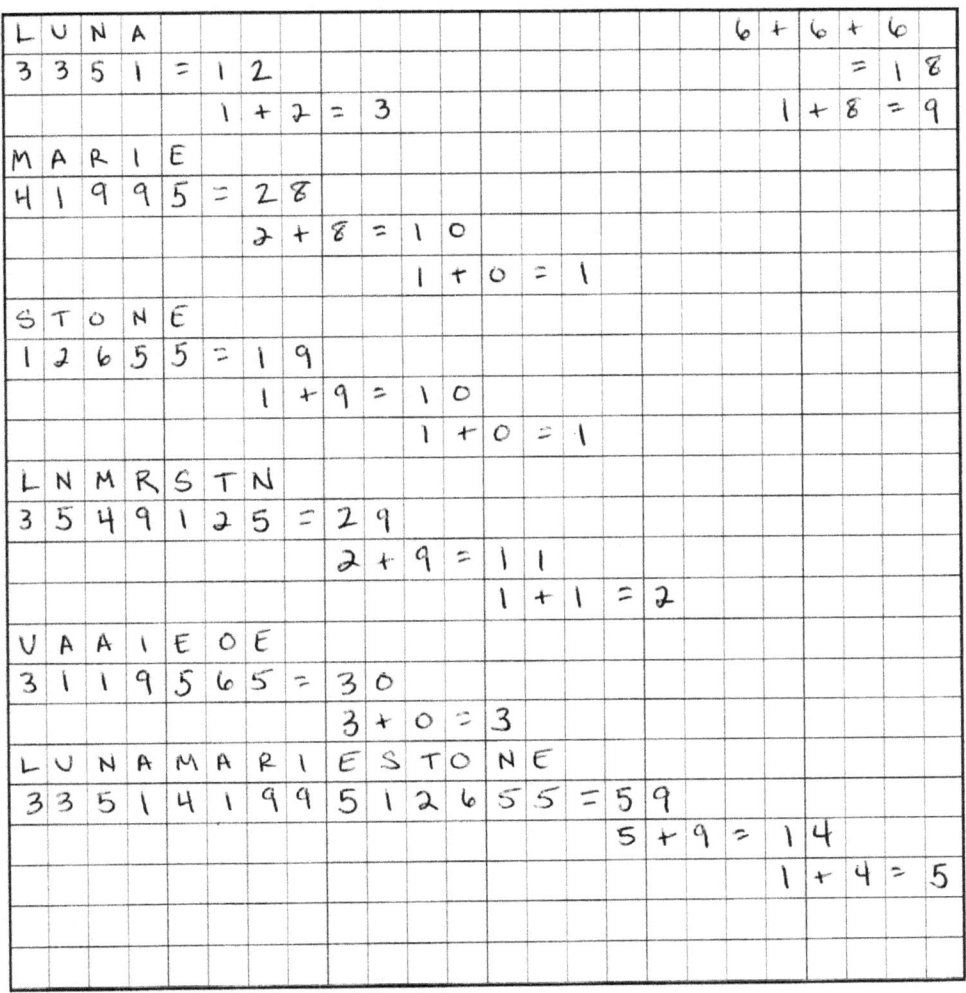

L	U	N	A											6	+	6	+	6	
3	3	5	1	=	1	2											=	1	8
				1	+	2	=	3							1	+	8	=	9
M	A	R	I	E															
H	1	9	9	5	=	2	8												
					2	+	8	=	1	0									
						1	+	0	=	1									
S	T	O	N	E															
1	2	6	5	5	=	1	9												
					1	+	9	=	1	0									
						1	+	0	=	1									
L	N	M	R	S	T	N													
3	5	4	9	1	2	5	=	2	9										
						2	+	9	=	1	1								
							1	+	1	=	2								
U	A	A	I	E	O	E													
3	1	1	9	5	6	5	=	3	0										
						3	+	0	=	3									
L	U	N	A	M	A	R	I	E	S	T	O	N	E						
3	3	5	1	4	1	9	9	5	1	2	6	5	5	=	5	9			
											5	+	9	=	1	4			
												1	+	4	=	5			

1	2	3	4	5	6	7	8	9
A	B	C	D	E	F	G	H	I
J	K	L	M	N	O	P	Q	R
S	T	U	V	W	X	Y	Z	

Life Path Number = Full Birthdate

Personality Number = Full name consonants

Soul Number = Full Name Vowels

Destiny Number = Full Name Complete

Cosmic Signature

of ___Luna_____

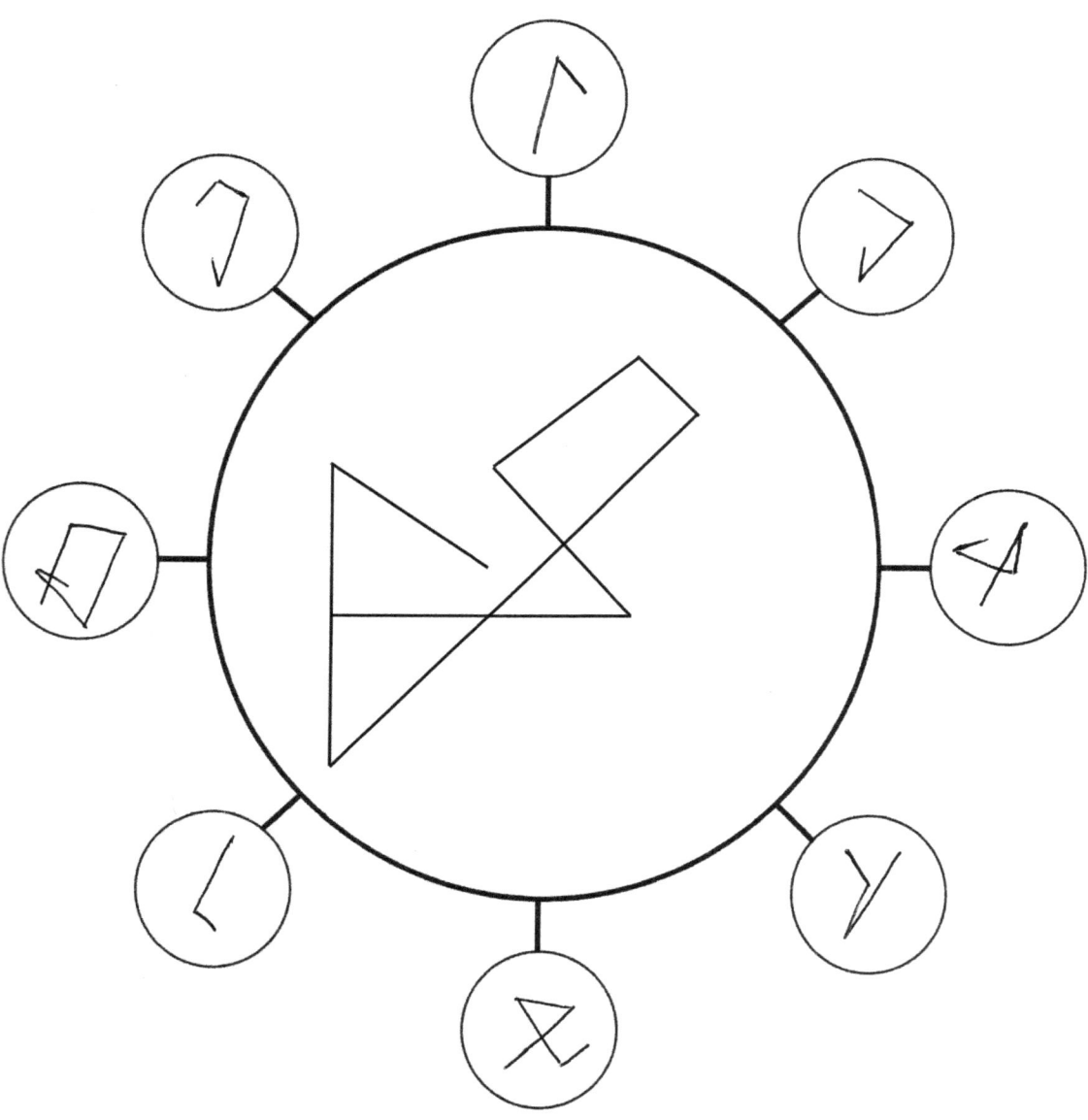

The Sigil of Self

of _____ Luna _____

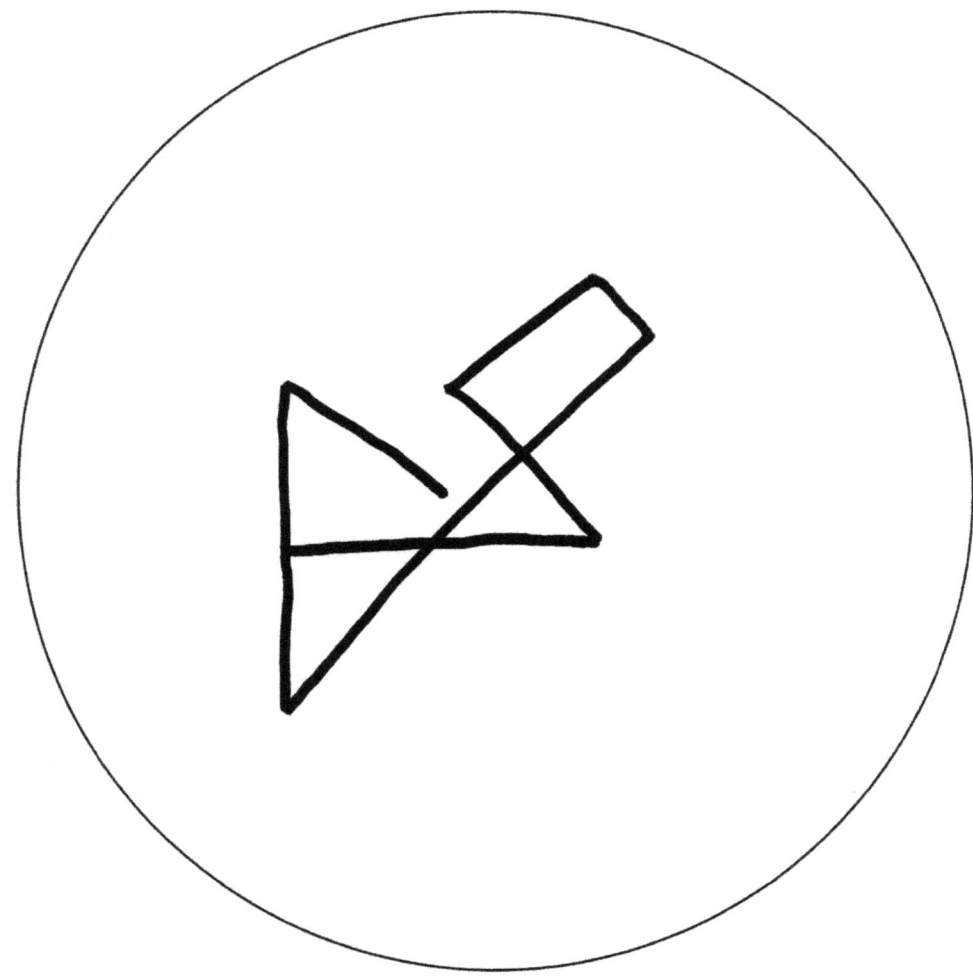

Example Digitized Version

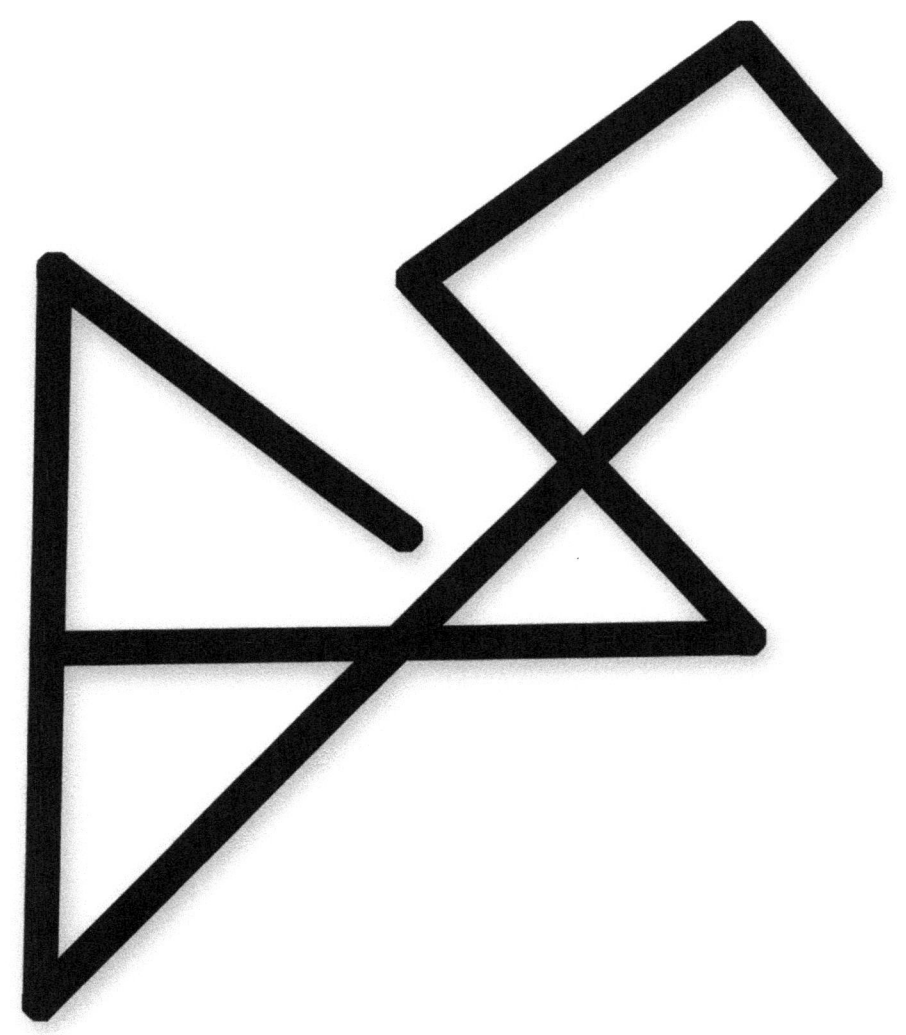

www.ingramcontent.com/pod-product-compliance
Lightning Source LLC
Chambersburg PA
CBHW041514120626
46551CB00018B/2428